Oracle RAC & Grid Tuning with Solid State Disk

Expert Secrets for High Performance Clustered Grid Computing

Oracle In-Focus Series

Mike Ault
Donald K. Burleson

RAMPANT TECHPRESS

I dedicate this book to my Mother and Father-in-Law, Mary and Dr. Tom Hamilton (Ret.) who have provided encouragement and help during the 32 years I have been married to their daughter. I also want to dedicate this book to Susan, my wife of 32 years and to the greater glory of God who made all of this possible.

- Mike Ault

I dedicate this book to my friends at Texas Memory Systems whose dedication to this experiment was instrumental in creating this book.

- Donald K Burleson

Oracle RAC & Grid Tuning with Solid State Disk

Expert Secrets for High Performance Clustered Grid Computing

By Mike Ault and Donald K. Burleson

Copyright © 2005 by Rampant TechPress. All rights reserved.

Printed in the United States of America.

Published in Kittrell, North Carolina, USA.

Oracle In-focus Series: Book #17

Series Editor: Don Burleson

Editors: Janet Burleson, John Lavender, and Robin Haden

Production Editor: Teri Wade

Cover Design: Bryan Hoff

Printing History: September, 2005 for First Edition

ISBN: 0-9761573-5-7

Library of Congress Control Number: 2005928017

Table of Contents

Using the Online Code Depot

Purchase of this book provides complete access to the online code depot that contains the sample code scripts. All of the code depot scripts in this book are available for download in zip format, ready to load and use and are located at the following URL:

rampant.cc/rac_ssd.htm

If technical assistance is needed with downloading or accessing the scripts, please contact Rampant TechPress at info@rampant.cc.

Are you WISE?

Get the premier Oracle tuning tool. The Workload Interface Statistical Engine for Oracle provides unparallel capability for time-series Oracle tuning, unavailable nowhere else.

WISE supplements Oracle Enterprise Manager and it can quickly plot and spot performance signatures to allow you to see hidden trends, fast. WISE interfaces with STATSPACK or AWR to provide unprecedented proactive tuning insights. Get WISE. Download now!

www.wise-oracle.com

Get the Oracle Script Collection

This is the complete Oracle script collection from Mike Ault and Donald Burleson, the world's best Oracle DBA's.

Packed with over 500 ready-to-use Oracle scripts, this is the definitive collection for every Oracle professional DBA. It would take many years to develop these scripts from scratch, making this download the best value in the Oracle industry.

It's only $39.95 (less than 7 cents per script!). For immediate download go to:

www.oracle-script.com

Conventions Used in this Book

It is critical for any technical publication to follow rigorous standards and employ consistent punctuation conventions to make the text easy to read.

However, this is not an easy task. Within Oracle there are many types of notation that can confuse a reader. Some Oracle utilities such as STATSPACK and TKPROF are always spelled in CAPITAL letters, while Oracle parameters and procedures have varying naming conventions in the Oracle documentation. It is also important to remember that many Oracle commands are case sensitive, and are always left in their original executable form, and never altered with italics or capitalization.

Parameters - All Oracle parameters will be lowercase italics. Exceptions to this rule are parameter arguments that are commonly capitalized (KEEP pool, TKPROF), these will be left in ALL CAPS.

Variables – All PL/SQL program variables and arguments will also remain in lowercase italics (*dbms_job, dbms_utility*).

Tables & dictionary objects – All data dictionary objects are referenced in lowercase italics (*dba_indexes, v$sql*). This includes all *v$* and *x$* views (*x$kcbcbh, v$parameter*) and dictionary views (*dba_tables, user_indexes*).

SQL – All SQL is formatted for easy use in the code depot, and all SQL is displayed in lowercase. The main SQL terms (select, from, where, group by, order by, having) will always appear on a separate line.

Programs & Products – All products and programs that are known to the author are capitalized according to the vendor specifications (IBM, DBXray, etc). All names known by Rampant TechPress to be trademark names appear in this text as initial caps.　References to UNIX are always made in uppercase.

Acknowledgements

I would like to acknowledge my co-author Don Burleson for his help and assistance in writing this book. I would also like to acknowledge Janet Burleson, John Lavender and Linda Webb at Rampant Technical Press for their invaluable aid. I would also like to thank Bert Scalzo and Claudia Fernandez at Quest for providing the Benchmark Factory program. Finally, and last but not least, thanks to Teri Wade and Robin Haden for their invaluable tech editing and pulling of the final manuscript into something worthwhile.

Mike Ault

This type of highly technical reference book requires the dedicated efforts of many people. Even though we are the authors, our work ends when we deliver the content. After each chapter is delivered, experienced copy editors polish the grammar and syntax.

The finished work is then reviewed as page proofs and turned over to the production manager, who arranges the creation of the online code depot and manages the cover art, printing, distribution, and warehousing. In short, the authors played a small role in the development of this book, and we need to thank and acknowledge everyone who helped bring this book to fruition:

- Teri Wade, for her hard work formatting the manuscript and producing the page proofs.

- Robin Haden, for her hard work copy editing the manuscript.

- Janet Burleson, for her production management, including the coordination of the cover art, page proofing, printing, and distribution.

- Mike Reed, for his superb cartoons.

With my sincere thanks,

Donald K Burleson

Preface

Technology is rapidly changing and those who get left behind will suffer the consequences. Almost every year new technology is introduced that changes the face of database systems and the advent of Solid-State Disk (SSD) appears to be one of the most important advances in database technology since the introduction of the relational database model.

The introduction of SSD is especially important to the Oracle professional because it changes the main tuning paradigm. Whereas the Oracle DBA of the 1990's was concerned with reducing disk I/O latency, this has now been removed with SSD, and the Oracle professional must learn a whole new way to manage and tune their Oracle databases.

This book shows how to leverage RAM-SAN technology to create Oracle RAC databases with blistering speed. You will learn proven techniques for leveraging RAM disk in an Oracle RAC and Grid environment including changes to initialization parameters and the selective use of SSD in large database environments including UNDO, REDO and TEMP tablespaces on solid-state disk.

This book shows actual TPC benchmark data and illustrates the high-bandwidth capabilities of SSD that revolutionize data retrieval engines.

- Learn the type of RAC and Grid databases that benefit the most from SSD solid-state technology.

- See real-world benefits for Oracle9i RAC and Oracle10g Grid systems with high-speed RAM-SAN.

- Understand how SSD facilitates performance improvements in RAC systems.

- Use proven techniques for the selective application of RAM disk in Oracle RAC.

- Explore how to tune an entire RAC or Grid Oracle database by speeding-up the I/O sub-system.

- Get a code depot of analysis scripts to see if solid-state disk is right for your Oracle RAC or Grid database.

It is our sincere hope that you will find the content from this book to be useful for your Oracle clustered database environment and that you will realize the benefits of solid-state disk with Oracle's Real Application Clusters.

Mike Ault
Don Burleson

Solid-State Disk with Oracle

Introduction

Today's world is one of constantly improving hardware technology. Yesterday's mainframe is today's PC, and there are unprecedented improvements to the speed and cost of computer hardware.   Moore's Law dictates that hardware costs will constantly fall while prices become constantly cheaper as shown in Figure 1.1.

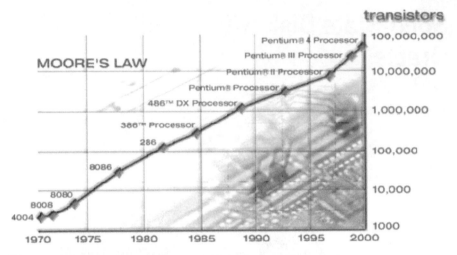

Figure 1.1: *Moore's Law circa 1975 (Source Intel)*

This rapid change is especially evident for Random Access Memory (RAM). Using RAM memory is critical to the performance of today's database management systems because RAM speed, expressed in nanoseconds, is more than 10,000 times faster than traditional disk storage device speed, expressed in milliseconds. RAM allows data to be accessed far faster than disk technology, and I/O-bound Oracle systems will soon be able to benefit from RAM like never before.

The latest incarnation of RAM storage devices are the solid-state disk (SSD) technology where the ancient spinning platters of magnetic coated media are replaced with an array of super fast solid-state RAM. Just like disks were backed up to tape, today's SSD devices achieve tertiary storage with software mechanisms that write the RAM frames to a back end disk on the device.

With the cost of SSD at only $1k/gig, many Oracle RAC systems are exploring how to leverage this powerful performance tool for their environment. Smaller databases can now run fully cached with SSD, yet there is a debate about the proper use of SSD in an Oracle environment.

Some IT managers cry about the high-cost of Solid-state disk.

The proper use of SSD is the central question for this benchmark. Traditional architectures of the 1990's have left users with duplicitous cache areas such as web cache, Oracle buffer cache, on-board disk cache, etc., and it is now the challenge of the Oracle DBA to exploit SSD for the most benefit for their database application.

This benchmark information will include the following sections:

- **Introduction to the issue:** There is a huge debate about the effect of data caching, with many opposing theories and conflicting research results. This section will take an objective look at the caching issue for Oracle databases.

- **Hypothesis:** This section will predict what the Oracle SSD TPC-C benchmark on RAC might reveal and justify the basis for the choice of testing scenarios.

- **Methodology:** This section describes the TPC-C database environment and hardware choices.

- **Results:** This section contains the results for 21 tests.

- **Conclusions:** This section compares predicted results with the associated hypothesis. The results will be extrapolated, and the benefits of SSD for specific types of Oracle database systems will be generalized.

The following section will introduce the current state of SSD research.

Introduction to Oracle Data Caching

Leveraging RAM resources has always been one of the central tasks of the Database Administrator (DBA). By definition, almost all databases are I/O intensive, and minimizing the expensive physical disk I/O has always been a major priority to ensure acceptable performance. Historically, RAM has been a scarce and expensive resource, and the DBA was challenged to find the best working set of highly used data to cache on their precious RAM media.

However, RAM is quite different than other hardware. Unlike CPU speed, which improves every year, RAM speed is constrained by the physics of silicon technology. Instead of speed improvements, there has been a constant decline in price. CPU speed also continues to outpace RAM speed. This means that RAM subsystems must be localized to keep the CPU's running at full capacity.

In the 1980's, a billion bytes of RAM cost over a million dollars; whereas, today one gigabyte of high-speed RAM storage can be acquired for less than $300.00. As a reference point, a billion bytes of RAM is equal to 1 Gigabyte. Some other pricing data points are outlined in Table 1.1 below:

YEAR	PRICE PER GBYTE TO ADD MEMORY TO SOLID STATE DISK (Texas Memory Systems)
1998	$9,000 (TMS)
1999	$6,000 (TMS)
2000	$5,000 (TMS)
2001	$5,000 (TMS)
2002	$3,000 (TMS)
2003	$2,500 (TMS)
2004	$1,500 (TMS)

Table 1.1: *RAM pricing data points*

Historically, RAM I/O bandwidth grows one bit every 18 months, making the first decade of the 21st Century the era of 64-bit RAM technology as shown in Table 1.2:

YEAR	RAM I/O BANDWIDTH SIZES
1970's	8 bit
1980's	16 bit
1990's	32 bit
2000's	64 bit
2020's	128 bit

Table 1.2: *RAM I/O bandwidth sizes*

Code Depot Username = reader, Password = performance

The bandwidth information is interesting. These numbers typically have as much to do with matching the bus width of the computer as they do with the speed of the RamSan chip. It is also more commonly used to describe SIMM performance as 8 bit/16/32/64 bit, so it might not be a good measure of chip performance. The data in Table 1.3 below was taken from a Kingston Memory webpage. It was part of their ultimate guide to memory:

YEAR	MEMORY TYPE	ACCESS TIME
1987	FPM	50ns
1995	EDO	50ns
1997	SDRAM	15ns
1998	SDRAM	10ns
1999	SDRAM	7.5ns
2000	DDR SDRAM	3.75ns
2001	DDR SDRAM	3ns
2002	DDR SDRAM	2.3ns
2003	DDR SDRAM	2ns

Table 1.3: *The Kingston Memory guide to memory*

It is clear that the dramatic decreases in RAM prices are going to change Oracle RAC database architectures. With RAM a once scarce and expensive resource, the Oracle DBA had to spend a huge amount of time managing Oracle memory allocation and optimization. This is about to change.

Today 128 gigabytes of SSD (i.e. Texas Memory Systems) can be purchased for about $150,000. By 2007, a Gigabyte of RAM is expected to cost much less. Of course, less expensive solid state disks will mean a dramatic change in Oracle database architecture as the old-fashioned model of disk-based data management will be abandoned in favor of a cache-based approach.

According to David Ensor, Oracle tuning expert, author, and Former Vice President of the Oracle Corporation's Performance Group, the increase in CPU power has shifted the bottleneck of many systems to disk I/O.

"Increased server power has meant that disk I/O has replaced CPU power and memory as the limiting factors on throughput for almost all applications and clustering is not a cost-effective way of increasing I/O throughput."

SSD as an Oracle Tuning Tool

The dramatic price/performance ratio of SSD is changing the way that Oracle databases are tuned. Suboptimal Oracle databases no longer have to undergo expensive and time consuming redesign, and SSD technology is now competing head-on with Oracle consulting services.

For example, a poorly designed Oracle database might take six months and over $500,000 in consulting costs to repair. If SSD is used as a remedy, the entire database will run more than ten times faster within 24 hours, at a fraction of the cost of repairing the source code.

Fighting excessive disk I/O has always been a problem!

Of course, the code still runs sub-optimally, but the performance complaints are quickly alleviated at a very competitive cost.

SSD promises to radically change the way that Oracle databases are managed, and users must understand the best approach to using this powerful new tool within their Oracle architecture.

RAM Access Speed with Oracle Databases

Now that inexpensive SSD is available, Oracle professionals are struggling to understand how to leverage this new hardware for their databases. The nature of Oracle RAM caching and why it is such an important issue will be covered in sections on:

- The history of Oracle RAM data buffering

- The problem is duplicitous RAM caches

- The issue of expensive logical I/O

Once the existing research has been reviewed, it will be possible to gain insights into the best placement for SSD in an Oracle environment.

The History of Oracle RAM data buffering

When Oracle was first introduced in the early 1990's, RAM was very expensive and few databases could afford to run large data buffer regions. Because RAM was such a limited resource, Oracle utilized a least frequently used algorithm within the data buffer to ensure that only the most frequently referenced data remained in the data buffer cache.

As of Oracle10g, seven separate RAM data buffers are available to hold incoming data blocks. These RAM areas define RAM space for incoming data blocks and are governed by the following Oracle10g parameters. The sum of all of these parameter values determines the total space reserved for Oracle data blocks.

- *db_cache_size*

- *db_keep_cache_size*

- *db_recycle_cache_size*

- *db_2k_cache_size*

- *db_4k_cache_size*

- *db_8k_cache_size*

- *db_16k_cache_size*

- *db_32k_cache_size*

Figure 1.2 below shows the plot of the relationship between the size of the RAM data buffers and physical disk reads. Clearly, there is a non-linear nature of RAM scalability for Oracle.

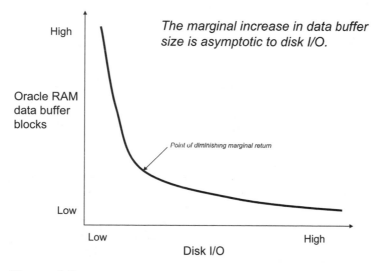

Figure 1.2: *The relationship between physical disk I/O and the size of the RAM buffer cache*

This relationship can be expressed mathematically as:

```
RAM Buffer Size = n/Physical reads
Where n = an observed constant
```

This relationship is the basis of the Automatic Memory Management (AMM) features of Oracle10g. Because the Automatic Workload Repository (AWR) is polling the efficiency of the data buffer, the AMM component can compute the point of diminishing marginal returns and reassign SGA RAM resources to ensure optimal sizing for all seven of the Oracle10g data buffers. In Calculus, the point of diminishing marginal returns is the second derivative of the equation.

Oracle uses this data to dynamically adjust each of the seven data buffers to keep them at their optimal size. In AMM, Oracle 10g uses the AWR to collect historical buffer utilization information and stores the buffer advisory information in the *dba_hist_db_cache_advice* view and offers a host of *dba_hist* views for Oracle RAM management as shown in Figure 1.3 below.

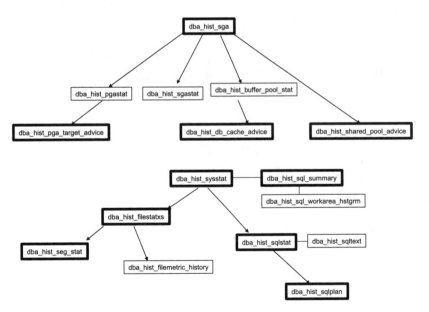

Figure 1.3: *Oracle10g dba_hist views for AMM*

When there is not enough RAM to cache the frequently used working set of data blocks, additional RAM is very valuable. Figure 1.4 shows that a small increase in RAM results in a large decrease in disk I/O.

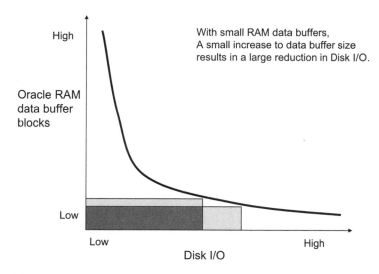

Figure 1.4: *Too small data buffers show large marginal reduction of disk I/O*

Traditionally, the optimal size of the Oracle RAM data buffer cache has been the point where the marginal benefit begins to decline, as measured by the acceleration of the curve denoted in Figure 1.4.

However, this marginal benefit does not last forever. As the Oracle database approaches full caching, it takes a relatively large amount of RAM to reduce physical disk I/O as shown in Figure 1.5. This is because rarely read data blocks are now being pulled into the SGA data buffers.

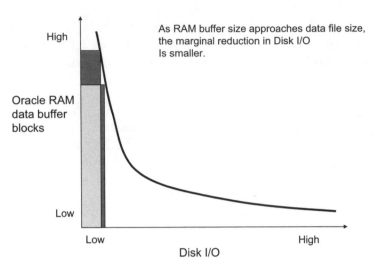

Figure 1.5: *The diminishing value of RAM buffering approaching full caching*

This optimal point is easily calculated with the Oracle10g AMM utility. The following script to display the output from the Oracle *v$db_cache_advice* utility will show how it works:

```
column c1    heading 'Cache Size (m)'      format 999,999,999,999
column c2    heading 'Buffers'             format 999,999,999
column c3    heading 'Estd Phys|Read Factor' format 999.90
column c4    heading 'Estd Phys| Reads'    format 999,999,999

select
   size_for_estimate          c1,
   buffers_for_estimate       c2,
   estd_physical_read_factor  c3,
   estd_physical_reads        c4
from
   v$db_cache_advice
where
   name = 'DEFAULT'
and
   block_size  = (SELECT value FROM V$PARAMETER
                  WHERE name = 'db_block_size')
and
   advice_status = 'ON';
```

Executing this utility will clearly show the relationship between the RAM buffer size and physical reads. The values range from ten percent of the current size to double the current size of the *db_cache_size*.

Cache Size (MB)	Buffers	Estd Phys Read Factor	Estd Phys Reads	
30	3,802	18.70	192,317,943	← 10% size
60	7,604	12.83	131,949,536	
91	11,406	7.38	75,865,861	
121	15,208	4.97	51,111,658	
152	19,010	3.64	37,460,786	
182	22,812	2.50	25,668,196	
212	26,614	1.74	17,850,847	
243	30,416	1.33	13,720,149	
273	34,218	1.13	11,583,180	
304	38,020	1.00	10,282,475	Current Size
334	41,822	.93	9,515,878	
364	45,624	.87	8,909,026	
395	49,426	.83	8,495,039	
424	53,228	.79	8,116,496	
456	57,030	.76	7,824,764	
486	60,832	.74	7,563,180	
517	64,634	.71	7,311,729	
547	68,436	.69	7,104,280	
577	72,238	.67	6,895,122	
608	76,040	.66	6,739,731	← 2x size

This predictive model is the basis for Oracle10g AMM. When the data from Oracle's predictive mode is plotted, the tradeoff becomes clear as shown in Figure 1.6.

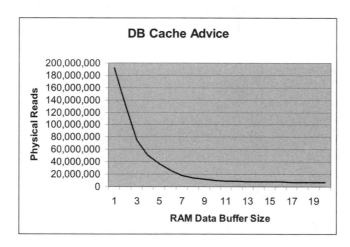

Figure 1.6: *A plot from the output of v$db_cache_advice*

The main point of this relationship between RAM buffering and physical reads is that all Oracle databases have data that is accessed with differing frequencies. In sum, the larger the working set of frequently referenced data blocks, the greater the benefit from speeding up block access.

Taking this into consideration, the following section will show how to more intelligently apply this knowledge to the use of SSD for Oracle.

Allocating Oracle Objects into Multiple RAM Data Buffers

Since very few Oracle databases can afford the cost of full RAM caching, many rules of thumb have been developed for the segregation and isolation of cached objects. Some of these rules of thumb will yield clues about the best way to utilize SSD in a solid-state Oracle environment:

- **Segregate large-table full-table scans:** Tables that experience large-table full-table scans will benefit from the largest supported block size and should be placed in a tablespace with the largest block size.

- **Use the RECYCLE Pool:** If *db_cache_size* is not being set to the largest supported block size for the server, the *db_recycle_cache_size* parameter should not be used. Instead, a *db_32k_cache_size,* or whatever the user's max is, should be created and all tables that experience frequent large-table full-table scans should be assigned to the largest buffer cache in the database.

- **Segregate Indexes:** In many cases, Oracle SQL statements will retrieve index information via an index range scan, scanning the b-tree or bitmap index for ranges of values that match the SQL search criteria. Hence, it is beneficial to have as much of an index residing in RAM as possible. One of the first things the Oracle 9i DBA should do is to migrate all of their Oracle indexes into a large blocksize tablespace. Indexes will always favor the largest supported blocksize.

- **Segregate random access reads:** For those databases that fetch small rows randomly from the disk, the Oracle DBA can segregate these types of tables into 2K tablespaces. While disk is becoming cheaper every day, it is still not wise to waste any available RAM by reading in more information to RAM than is actually going bc used by the query. Hence, many Oracle DBAs will use small block size is in cases of tiny, random access record retrieval.

- **Segregate LOB column tables:** For those Oracle tables that contain raw, long raw, or in-line LOBs, moving the table rows to large block size will have an extremely beneficial effect on disk I/O. Experienced DBAs will check *dba_tables.avg_row_len* to make sure that the blocksize is larger than the average size. Row chaining will be reduced while at the same time the entire LOB can be read within a single disk I/O, thereby avoiding the additional overhead of having Oracle to go out of read multiple blocks.

- **Segregate large-table full-table scan rows:** When the recycle pool was first introduced in Oracle8i, the idea was the full-table scan data blocks, which are not likely to be reread by other transactions, could be quickly flushed through the Oracle SGA thereby reserving critical RAM for those data blocks which are likely to be reread by another transaction. In Oracle9i, the RECYCLE pool can be configured to use a smaller block size.

- **Check the average row length:** The block size for a table's tablespace should always be greater than the average row length for the table, *dba_tables.avg_row_len*. Not only is it smaller than the average row length, rows chaining occurs and excessive disk I/O is incurred.

- **Use large blocks for data sorting:** The TEMP tablespace will benefit from the largest supported blocksize. This allows disk sorting to happen in large blocks with a minimum of disk I/O.

These suggestions are very important to the study of the best way to utilize SSD as an alternative caching mechanism.

However, recent TPC-C benchmarks make it clear that very large RAM regions are a central component in high performance Oracle databases. The 2004 UNISYS Oracle Windows benchmark exceeded 250,000 transactions per minute using a Windows-based 16-CPU server with 115 gigabytes of Oracle data buffer cache. The following are the Oracle parameters that were used in the benchmark, and the benefit of large scale RAM caching is clear:

- $db\_16k\_cache\_size$ = 15010M

- $db\_8k\_cache\_size$ = 1024M

- db_cache_size = 8096M

- $db\_keep\_cache\_size$ = 78000M

At this point, it is very clear that RAM resources are an important factor in maintaining the performance of I/O intensive Oracle systems.

Monitoring Oracle can be very time-consuming.

Improving I/O Speed is Not a Silver Bullet

SSD and RAM buffer caching are only important to I/O-intensive Oracle databases. If an Oracle database is constrained by other environmental factors such as CPU or network, speeding up the I/O subsystem will not result in any appreciable performance gains. To learn about databases resource bottlenecks, the DBA need only display the top-5 timed events from STATSPACK.

The following is a typical OLTP database where I/O delay is the main source of wait time. I/O comprises more than 70% of total elapsed time.

```
Top 5 Timed Events
~~~~~~~~~~~~~~~~~~                                      % Total
Event                         Waits        Time (s)    Ela Time
---------------------------   ------------ -----------  --------
db file sequential read       2,598        7,146          48.54
db file scattered read        25,519       3,246          22.04
library cache load lock       673          1,363           9.26
CPU time                      1,154        7.83            6.21
log file parallel write       19,157       837             5.68
```

Again, it is critical to note that additional RAM resources may not have any appreciable effect on databases that are not I/O intensive. For example, some scientific Oracle databases only

---

read a small set of experimental results and spend the majority of database time performing computations. The output of such a database is shown below:

```
Top 5 Timed Events
~~~~~~~~~~~~~~~~~~                                      % Total
Event                           Waits   Time (s) Ela Time
-------------------------------- ------------ ----------- --------
CPU time                        4,851      4,042   55.76
db file sequential read         1,968      1,997   27.55
log file sync                 299,097        369    5.08
db file scattered read         53,031        330    4.55
log file parallel write       302,680        190    2.62
```

In this example, CPU time is the primary source of database delay, and improving the speed of the I/O with SSD may not have an appreciable effect on overall Oracle performance.

One must be cognizant that it is foolish to focus solely on minimizing physical disk I/O. For databases with sub-optimal SQL statements, poor performance is commonly combined with a high data buffer cache hit ratio and little disk I/O. For these databases, the root cause of the performance problem is excessive logical I/O, whereby the sub-optimal SQL rereads data blocks over and over from the RAM data buffers.

There are several myths of Oracle physical I/O that must be exposed at this point:

- **All Oracle databases are I/O-bound:** Untrue. Databases with a reasonable data buffer cache size and a small working set will usually be constrained by CPU or network latency.

- **The Data Buffer Hit Ratio (DBHR) will yield caching efficiency:** Untrue, except in cases of a super small cache. The DBHR only measures the propensity that a data block will be in the buffer on the second I/O request.

- **Only faster disk can remove I/O bottlenecks:** Untrue. This is a common myth. There are other non-RAM approaches to reducing disk I/O for Oracle databases:

- **Adjusting *optimizer_mode*:** Oracle will generate widely differing SQL execution plans depending on the optimizer mode.

- **Re-analyze SQL Optimizer statistics:** Using better quality CBO statistics with *dbms_stats* and adding column histograms can make a huge difference in disk activity.

- **Adjusting Oracle parameters:** Resetting the *optimizer_index_cost_adj* and *optimizer_index_caching* parameters can affect physical reads

- **Improve *clustering_factor* for index range scans:** Manually resequence table rows to improve *clustering_factor*, sometimes using single-table clusters, can reduce disk I/O.

- **Use Materialized Views:** Systems with batch only updates may greatly benefit from Materialized Views to pre-join tables. Of course, the overhead of refresh commit is too great for high update systems.

With that information on the historical issues about how Oracle uses RAM, the next step is to look at the issues of duplicated RAM caching in large Oracle systems.

The Problem of Duplicitous RAM Caches

As hardware evolved though the 1990's, independent components of database systems started to employ their own RAM caching tools as shown in Figure 1.7.

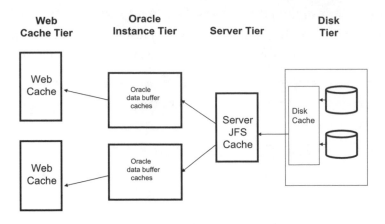

Figure 1.7: *Multiple RAM caches in an Oracle enterprise*

In this figure, it is clear that the Oracle database is not the only component to utilize RAM caching. The disk array employs a RAM cache, the servers has a Journal File System (JFS) RAM cache, and the front end web server also serve to cache Oracle data.

Older technology can be very dangerous

This concept is important because many enterprises may inadvertently double cache Oracle data. Even more problematic

---

are the fake statistics reported by Oracle when multiple level caches are employed:

- **Fake Physical I/O times:** When using a disk array with a built-in RAM cache, the disk I/O subsystem may acknowledge a physical write to Oracle when, in reality, the data has not yet been written to the physical disk spindle. This can skew timing of disk read/write speed.

- **Wasted Oracle Data Buffer RAM:** In systems that employ web servers, the Apache front end may cache frequently used data. Hence, significant Oracle resources may be wasted caching data blocks that are already cached on the web server tier.

The next section will cover the best way to use SSD in an Oracle RAC environment. The information begins with an examination of the relationship between physical disk I/O (POI) and Oracle Logical I/O (LIO).

Why is Oracle Logical I/O So Slow?

Disk latency is generally measured in milliseconds, while RAM access is expressed in nanoseconds. In theory, RAM is four orders of magnitude (10,000 times) faster than disk. However, this is not true when using Oracle. In practice, logical I/O is seldom more than 1,000 times faster than disk I/O. Most Oracle experts say that logical disk I/O is only 15 times to 100 times faster than a physical disk I/O.

Oracle has internal data protection mechanisms at work that cause a RAM data block access, a consistent get, to be far slower due to internal locks and latch serialization mechanisms. This overhead is required by Oracle to maintain read consistency and data concurrency.

If Oracle logical I/O is expensive, can this expense be avoided when reading directly from disk? The answer is important to the information presented about the most appropriate placement for SSD in an Oracle environment.

Super large disks are an issue to be noted. With 144 gigabyte disks becoming commonplace, I/O intensive database will often see disk latency because many tasks are competing to read blocks on different parts of the super large disk.

An Oracle physical read must read the disk data block and then transfer it into the Oracle RAM buffer before the data is passed to the requesting program as shown in Figure 1.8.

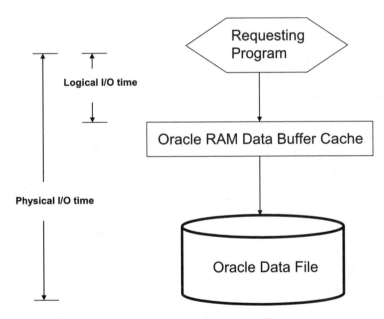

Figure 1.8: *Physical reads include logical I/O latency*

If one accepts that LIO expense is going to happen regardless of whether or not a PIO is performed, valuable insight into the proper placement for SSD in an Oracle environment is achieved.

Finding the Baselines

A critical point is Oracle databases are always changing, and the database that was examined at 10:00 AM may be completely different than the database examined at 3:00 PM. Does this mean that a broad brush application of SSD is not valid?

When the performance of Oracle disk I/O is examined over time periods, regular signatures appear when the I/O information is aggregated by hours-of-the-day and day-of-the-week as shown in Figure 1.9.

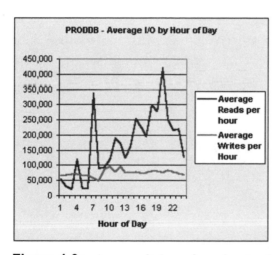

Figure 1.9: *Average disk reads and writes by hour-of-the-day*

Most Oracle professionals use Oracle9i STATSPACK or Oracle10g AWR information to gather these baselines. Once the repeating I/O trends have been identified, it will be possible to apply a broad brush to the use of SSD, placing the fast I/O devices where they will do the most good.

I/O information can be captured at the file level, and this can give insights into the best data files to place on super fast SSD.

The following script extracts the physical read information from the Oracle 10g *dba_hist_filestatxs* view:

```
break on begin_interval_time skip 2

column phyrds   format 999,999,999
column begin_interval_time format a25

select
   begin_interval_time,
   filename,
   phyrds
from
   dba_hist_filestatxs
  natural join
   dba_hist_snapshot
;
```

The result below shows a running total of physical reads by datafile. The snapshots are collected every half-hour. Starting from this script, a *where* clause criteria could easily be added resulting in a unique time-series exception report.

```
SQL> @reads

BEGIN_INTERVAL_TIME        FILENAME                                   PHYRDS
-------------------------  ----------------------------------------  -------
24-FEB-04 11.00.32.000 PM  E:\ORACLE\ORA92\FSDEV10G\SYSTEM01.DBF     164,700
                           E:\ORACLE\ORA92\FSDEV10G\UNDOTBS01.DBF     26,082
                           E:\ORACLE\ORA92\FSDEV10G\SYSAUX01.DBF     472,008
                           E:\ORACLE\ORA92\FSDEV10G\USERS01.DBF        1,794
                           E:\ORACLE\ORA92\FSDEV10G\T_FS_LSQ.ORA       2,123


24-FEB-04 11.30.18.296 PM  E:\ORACLE\ORA92\FSDEV10G\SYSTEM01.DBF     167,809
                           E:\ORACLE\ORA92\FSDEV10G\UNDOTBS01.DBF     26,248
                           E:\ORACLE\ORA92\FSDEV10G\SYSAUX01.DBF     476,616
                           E:\ORACLE\ORA92\FSDEV10G\USERS01.DBF        1,795
                           E:\ORACLE\ORA92\FSDEV10G\T_FS_LSQ.ORA       2,244


25-FEB-04 12.01.06.562 AM  E:\ORACLE\ORA92\FSDEV10G\SYSTEM01.DBF     169,940
                           E:\ORACLE\ORA92\FSDEV10G\UNDOTBS01.DBF     26,946
                           E:\ORACLE\ORA92\FSDEV10G\SYSAUX01.DBF     483,550
                           E:\ORACLE\ORA92\FSDEV10G\USERS01.DBF        1,799
                           E:\ORACLE\ORA92\FSDEV10G\T_FS_LSQ.ORA       2,248
```

Of course, a little tweaking to the script could result in a report on physical writes, read time, write time, single block reads, and a host of other interesting metrics from the *dba_hist_filestatxs* view.

RAC and SSD

What is unique about RAC and SSD? RAC introduces a new source of latency into the I/O picture. This new source of latency deals with the cluster interconnect. As the latency of the cluster interconnect increases, the ability to scale as well as the performance of the cached data decreases. This decrease in performance is especially noticeable in the case where all of the application data is cached across the virtual memory area afforded by Oracle10g RAC.

Given this new source of latency, the effects of the cluster interconnect in a fully cached environment must be considered. Is the interconnect latency less than the latency of the SSD? Is the interconnect latency higher than the SSD latency? These are critical questions that will determine whether or not to force cache transfer or force reads from the SSD as the primary means of cache replacement for data. In all but the fastest interconnects, SSD is faster.

What does SSD being faster than the interconnect for data transfer indicate? Believe it or not, better performance may be achieved by forcing the old disk ping behavior instead of a transfer across the interconnect! Oracle has optimized the I/O path more thoroughly than the memory paths taken by RAC in a transfer situation, thus if the old slow disks are replaced with SSD technology, better performance may result from reading from the SSD! This behavior will be examined in the TPC-C results chapter.

The next step is to review the existing research on SSD and see that other Oracle experts say about using SSD with Oracle.

A Review of Existing SSD Research Findings

Different researchers are coming to different conclusions about the applicability of SSD to Oracle systems. There are three research papers on SSD, and each arrives at similar conclusions about the use of SSD with Oracle. Complete references are included in the reference section. The following sections provide a quick look at the summary findings from each study.

The top Oracle Experts have examined SSD technology

James Morle

According to Morle in 2002, SSD is great for Oracle redo logs, undo tablespace, rollback segment tablespace in Oracle8i, and the TEMP tablespace. He notes that for rollback segments, SSD is a great help:

> "This is where SSD can help out. By deploying a single SSD, all redo logs can be located away from the RAID 1+0 array, whilst providing low latency writes and high bandwidth reads (for archiving)."

Morle also asserts that full caching of a database on SSD may not improve performance:

"If the whole database were running from SSD, there would be enormous pieces of unnecessary work going on, such as:

Management of the buffer cache

Context switches into kernel mode to perform I/O

Conversion of the request into SCSI/Fibre Channel

Transmission across the SAN

And all the way back again

In comparison to disk I/O, this whole process is stunningly fast. In comparison to just reading the data straight from user space memory, however, it is incredibly slow!"

Morle notes that a typical OLTP system has a working set of frequently referenced data blocks, and those might be good candidates for SSD. For DSS and Data Warehouse systems, Morle advocates moving the current table partitions onto SSD devices, leaving the others on traditional disk.

Dr. Paul Dorsey

In another landmark SSD study in 2004, Dr. Paul Dorsey showed that the data transfer rates for SSD's are always better than traditional disk:

DEVICE	TEST#1: BUFFERED READ	TEST #2: SEQUENTIAL READ	TEST #3: RANDOM READ	TEST #4: BUFFERED WRITE	TEST #5: SEQUENTIAL WRITE	TEST #6: RAMDOM WRITE
RamSan	95	98	98	86	84	82
IDE	85	40	6	65	38	11
SCSI	65	33	9	49	33	11

Dr. Dorsey concludes:

> "Technologically, SSD is one of the best sources of performance improvement for an Oracle database if you have a typical OLTP system including many transactions which access different small amounts of random data and lots of users.
>
> SSDs may also improve data warehouse applications because of the improved query performance. There is no generic answer for all questions, but solid state disks represent another way of thinking about managing enterprise-wide databases. "

Woody Hutsell

The Texas Memory Systems whitepaper titled *Faster Oracle Database Access with the RAMSAN-210* (Hutsell, 2001) concludes that certain types of Oracle databases will always benefit from SSD:

There are some databases that should have all of their files moved to SSD. These databases tend to have at least one of the following characteristics:

- **High concurrent access**: DBA's managing databases that are being hit by a large number of concurrent users should consider storing all of their data on SSD. This will ensure that storage is not a bottleneck for the application and maximize the utilization of servers and networks. I/O wait time will be minimized and servers and bandwidth will be fully utilized.

- **Frequent random accesses to all tables**: For some databases, it is impossible to identify a subset of files that are frequently accessed. Many times these databases are effectively large indices.

- **Small to medium size databases**: Given the fixed costs associated with buying RAID systems, it is often economical to buy a SSD to store small to medium sized databases. A RamSan-210, for example, can provide 32GB of database storage for the price of some enterprise RAID systems.

Conclusion

The research indicates that SSD can be very valuable to Oracle databases, with the total benefit depending on the type of processing characteristics.

- **Use SSD for high-impact files**: Experts agree that Oracle redo log files, undo segment and temporary tablespace file will greatly benefit from SSD.

- **SSD has impressive speed improvements**: Dorsey reported a 67% gain (.67x) in data access speed with SSD. Morle noted a reported a 25% (.25x) increase in system speed with SSD

- **SSD may shift the Oracle bottleneck to CPU**: SSD should only be attempted when CPU consumption, as measured by a STATSPACK top-5 wait event report, is less than 50% of the consumption. Using SSD will shift the bottleneck from I/O to CPU, and the server may require more CPU's to improve dispatching, or faster CPU's, e.g. Itanium2 processors.

- **Read intensive system benefit most from SSD**: Write intensive systems, especially those with high buffer invalidations, may only see a marginal speed improvement.

- **SSD will speed up access on super large disks**: The 114 gigabyte disk often experience disk enqueue as competing tasks wait their turn at the read-write heads. SSD will surely improve throughput for these types of database disks.

SSD Benchmark Hypothesis

Now that the issues surrounding SSD in an Oracle environment have been covered, one can form a hypothesis about the results of the benchmark tests.

Mike Ault develops an SSD test plan

The central question of this study is to determine the benefit of SSD for Oracle under these conditions:

- **No SSD with a super large Oracle data buffer:** This can minimize PIO with only one physical read into the data buffer, but LIO overhead will be revealed.

- **SSD with a tiny Oracle data buffer:** This makes PIO faster but will have repeated LIO overhead as data blocks are aged out of the Oracle data buffer. The LIO overhead would be expected to be huge, with high latch contention, buffer busy waits, and free buffer waits.

- **SSD for files with large Oracle Data buffer cache:** This is duplicating RAM, but it would relieve the LIO issue.

It is now possible to postulate about the benchmark results. If it is assumed that SSD is far faster for PIO, the issue of duplicitous Oracle activity remains. At PIO time, the data block must still be read into the *db_cache_size,* and then a consistent get is required to deliver the data block to the requesting program.

RAM resources, therefore, appear to be better allocated directly to the *db_cache_size* instead of using the RAM with SSD.

Specific Architectures

Large data buffers with SSD for:

- Redo log files
- Undo segments
- Temporary tablespace blocks

The next chapter will provide a look at the benchmark study that was created specifically to test these hypotheses and show conclusively how Oracle RAC functions with SSD.

References:

- Dorsey, P, *Solid State Disks: Sorting out the Myths from the Reality*, IOUG SELECT Magazine (2004)

- Morle, J, *Solid State Disks in an Oracle Environment: The New Rules of Deployment*, Scale Abilities Ltd., 2002.

- Hutsell, W, *Faster Oracle Database Access with the RAMSAN-210*, Texas Memory Systems,

- http://www.storagesearch.com/texasmemsysart1.pdf

SSD and Bandwidth

"It looks like a disk bandwidth problem".

Bandwidth and Oracle I/O

It should not be a surprise that the vast majority of Oracle databases are I/O centric, serving-up billions of bytes of information to the application layer. Even with the rapidly-falling costs of RAM, large Oracle databases may perform millions of disk reads per minute, and the I/O subsystem is the source of system-wide bottlenecks.

Over the past decade, Oracle has developed sophisticated caching mechanisms to minimize disk I/O, but managing I/O throughput remains a major issue. There are several non-Oracle components that are used to optimize data-centric applications:

Operating Systems – The RedHat Linux 4.0 operating system is specifically optimized for use by Oracle database, with special attention to the I/O drivers.

Hardware – Several vendors now offer servers that are architected to maximize I/O throughput. For example, the UNISS ES-7000 series of servers use Non Uniform Memory Access (NUMA) to achieve optimal I/O in a data-centric environment.

Solid-state Disk (SSD) – SSD, one of the greatest tools for achieving high data concurrency, is RAM disk that allows high bandwidth and data transfer rates that are an order of magnitude faster than the old-fashioned spinning platter devices.

Preventing disk I/O bottlenecks has always been one of the central tasks of the Oracle Database Administrator (DBA). By definition, almost all Oracle databases are I/O intensive and minimizing the expensive physical disk I/O has always been a major priority to ensure acceptable performance. The only exceptions are scientific applications such as Laboratory Information Management Systems (LIMS), which read a small data set and perform CPU-intensive calculations.

The History of I/O Bandwidth

Historically, RAM I/O bandwidth grows one bit every 18 months, making the first decade of the 21st Century the era of 64-bit RAM technology:

1970's	8 bit
1980's	16 bit
1990's	32 bit
2000's	64 bit
2010's	28 bit

As of 2006, the vast majority of hardware vendors (Sun, HP, IBM, UNISYS and Dell) offer 64-bit servers with far higher bandwidth than their ancient 32-bit predecessors.

However, RAM is quite different from other computer hardware such as disk and CPU. Unlike CPU speed, which improves every year, RAM speed is constrained by the physics of silicon technology. Instead of speed improvements, there is a constant decline in price. CPU speed also continues to outpace RAM speed and this means that RAM sub-systems must be localized to keep the CPUs running at full capacity.

"Moore's Law" states that CPU speed will constantly improve while process costs fall. Unfortunately, this is not the case for RAM and disk, and Figure 2.1 shows that the "real" disk speeds have not improved significantly in the past 15 years:

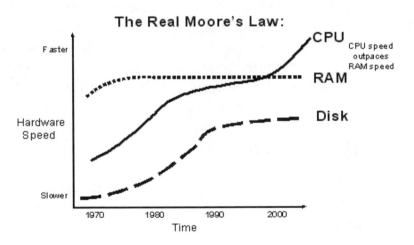

Figure 2.1: *CPU speed outpaces Disk and RAM speed*

As shown in Figure 2.1 CPU speed continues to double every few years, while the speed of disk and RAM cannot boast such a rapid rate of speed improvements.

For RAM, the speed has increase from 50 nanoseconds (one billionth of a second) to two nanoseconds, a 25x improvement over a 30-year period. At access speeds of two-billionths of a second, today's DDR SDRAM is stressing the limits of silicon technology, and it's unlikely that significantly faster speeds will be seen in the next decade (Table 2.1).

Year	RAM Type	Access Speed
1987	FPM	50ns
1995	EDO	50ns
1997	SDRAM	15ns
1998	SDRAM	10ns
1999	SDRAM	7.50 ns
2000	DDR SDRAM	3.75 ns
2001	DDR SDRAM	3.00 ns
2002	DDR SDRAM	2.30 ns
2003	DDR SDRAM	2.00 ns

Table 2.1: *RAM speed over time*

It is very clear than CPU speed will continue to outpace RAM speed and this has important ramifications for Oracle database processing. The advent of Non-Uniform Memory Access (NUMA) is predicated on the fact that data storage (RAM) must be localized as close to the CPU as possible to maximize throughput (Figure 2.2):

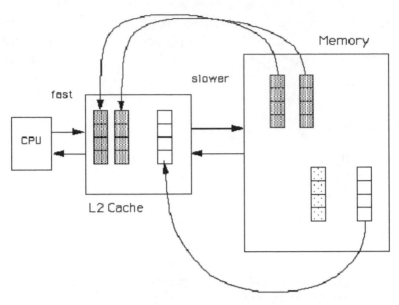

Figure 2.2: *The NUMA architecture for Oracle*

NUMA has been available for years in high-end UNIX servers running SMP (symmetric multi-processor) configurations. The vendors know that NUMA technology allows for faster communication between the distributed RAM in a multi-processor server environment. NUMA is supported by Linux and Windows Advanced Server 2003 and is a feature of the Intel Itanium2 chipset, which is used in the latest Oracle server blades for Oracle Grid computing.

Oracle 10g has become NUMA-aware and the database engine can now exploit the high-speed L2 cache on the latest SMP servers. According to David Ensor, a recognized Oracle tuning expert, author, and Former Vice President of the Oracle Corporation's Performance Group, the inordinate increase in CPU power has shifted the bottleneck of many systems to disk I/O, as the disk technology fails to keep-up with CPU.

The chasm between bandwidth and performance

In addition to the growing gap between storage performance and processor performance is a similar chasm between bandwidth and storage performance. Bandwidth is becoming available at rates that exceed even the improvement in processor performance. Already today, there is a glut of bandwidth that is now available to enterprises for a much lower cost than was ever possible. With almost unlimited bandwidth, the demands on the remainder of the data center only intensify. From the firewall to storage, every aspect of system performance will need to be analyzed for bottlenecks.

Storage densities are increasing, and data access problems are only getting worse. Going forward, storage managers will be required to balance the need for capacity with the need for performance. There are no easy solutions to the problem if the options only include hard disk based JBOD or RAID systems. It is the mechanical aspect of hard drives that ensures they will always be much slower than the server or incapable of filling massive enterprise bandwidth.

The next section explores how these advances in hardware are shifting Oracle's processing bottlenecks.

The shift in Oracle bottlenecks

As noted in Chapter 1, the dramatic decrease in the cost of RAM is radically changing the Oracle database architecture. In 2005, 100 gigabytes of SSD (i.e. Texas Memory Systems) can be obtained for about $150,000.

Historically, RAM has been a scarce and expensive resource, and the DBA was challenged to find the data that was referenced most frequently to cache on precious RAM media.

This new age of cheap solid state disks has meant a dramatic change in Oracle database architecture, as the old fashioned model of disk-based data management is being abandoned in favor of a cache-based I/O approach.

For years, storage architects have observed the growing divide between processor performance and storage access times. Remember, when the CPU waits on storage, the users are waiting on storage.

According to a whitepaper by James Morle, SSD is great for high-bandwidth I/O components such as Oracle redo logs. The Oracle redo logs archive the row before images and they are used for data recovery in the event of a disk crash. Morle notes:

> "This is where SSD can help out. By deploying a single SSD, all redo logs can be located away from the RAID 1+0 array, whilst providing low latency writes and high bandwidth reads (for archiving)."

The next section looks at the inherent bandwidth limitations of platter-based disk storage so that a better understanding can get gained of the benefits of SSD for Oracle data files.

Bandwidth Limitations of Platter Disk

The limitations of the magnetic-coated disk platters have been well understood since they were first invented nearly a half century ago. Back in the day of *Data Processing,* disks were much smaller, and Oracle databases could get additional bandwidth by having the data files reside on multiple disk spindles with more disk controllers (Figure 2.3):

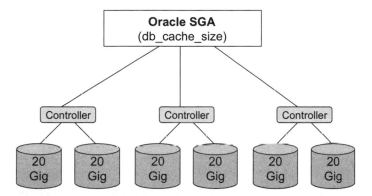

Figure 2.3: – *Multiple disk devices improves bandwidth*

The Problem of Super-large Disks

Over the decades, disk manufacturers continued to make disk devices larger, ignoring the bandwidth limitations imposed by locating all of the data storage on a single device. As of 2005, it is very difficult to purchase a disk spindle that is less than 100 gigabytes, and this causes disk I/O bandwidth issues at two levels (Figure 2.4):

- Bandwidth limitations within the disk as a result of excessive read-write head movement

- Controller bandwidth limitations

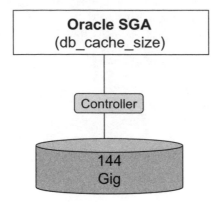

Figure 2-4: *Large disks can induce bandwidth limitations*

Today's super-large disks allow the Oracle DBA to place an entire database onto a single pair of mirrored devices. This imposes a severe data transmission bottleneck, especially when concurrent requests for data are made for data on different cylinders. This can cause the disk to shake like an unbalanced washing machine in the spin cycle, and seriously impede the ability of Oracle to deliver information to an application.

The next section will explore some methods for removing this technology imposed bandwidth limitation and see how SSD can increase throughput for almost all Oracle databases.

Removing Bandwidth Saturation with SSD

DBA's who are experiencing Oracle RAC databases that are being hit by a large number of concurrent users should consider storing all concurrent access data files on SSD. This will make sure that storage is not a bottleneck for the application and maximize the utilization of servers and networks. I/O wait time will be minimized and servers and bandwidth will be fully utilized.

For example, the Texas Memory Systems RamSan has 3,000 MB per second bandwidth and 250,000 I/Os per second sustained which means that it can simultaneously boost performance for multiple servers. The RamSan-320 uses a three-disk RAID back-up system, in addition to internal batteries, component redundancy, and hot-swap capabilities, for added data protection. This is a significant advance in reliability for 24 X 7 data center operations with critical applications.

There are two main benefits to having high bandwidth:

- Some RAC applications require high bandwidth. Good examples include Oracle RAC video-on-demand databases where thousands of users must access the video files in different spots.

- High bandwidth enables the SSD to be shared across multiple hosts without impacting performance. This feature is critical for Oracle RAC systems.

It is important to remember that there is one huge difference between disk and SSD. Solid state disks have the high bandwidth to sustain random data streams while traditional platter disks can only sustain high bandwidth numbers with sequential data streams (Figure 2.5).

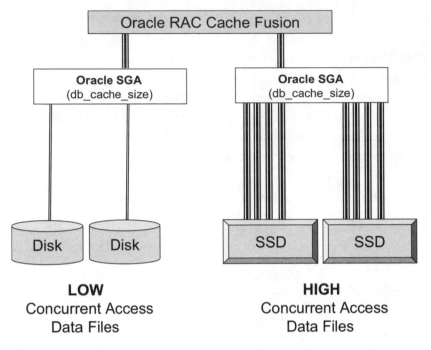

Figure 2.5: *SSD vs. disk bandwidth in Oracle RAC*

I/O bandwidth can be conceptualized as the width of the highway between the device and the Oracle SGA. Traditional disk is a one lane dirt road while SSD is an eight lane superhighway.

The RAM-to-RAM transfer of SSD to the Oracle RAC data buffer cache can have hundreds of times of the throughput of platter disks and can help ensure that the CPU's are fully utilized.

Oracle RAC Cache Fusion and I/O Bandwidth

Oracle RAC Cache Fusion uses a high-speed IPC interconnect to provide cache-to-cache transfers of data blocks between instances in a cluster. This is called data block shipping. This eliminates the disk I/O and optimizes read/write concurrency.

Block reads take advantage of the speed of IPC and an interconnecting network.

The cache-to-cache data transfer is performed through the high speed IPC interconnect. The Oracle Global Cache Service (GCS) tracks blocks that were shipped to other instances by retaining block copies in memory. Each such copy is called a past image (PI). The GCS, via the LMSx background process, tracks one or more past image versions (PI) for a block in addition to the traditional GCS resource roles and modes. In the event of a node failure, Oracle can reconstruct the current version of a block by using a saved PI.

Simultaneous Reads on Different RAC Nodes

Simultaneous reads of the same data block on multiple nodes cause bandwidth bottlenecks, but they can also cause cache conflicts within RAC. Real Application Clusters resolves this situation because multiple instances share the same blocks for read access without cache conflicts. Conflicts can only occur for read/write and write/write situations.

Simultaneous Reads and Writes on Different RAC Nodes

Simultaneous reads and writes on different nodes are the dominant form of concurrency problems in Online Transaction Processing (OLTP), hybrid OLTP, and data warehouse applications. A read of a data block that has been modified recently can be for either the current version of the block or for a read-consistent previous version. In both cases, the block will be transferred from one cache to the other via the high speed interconnect.

Simultaneous Writes on Different RAC Nodes

When one or more users need to modify the same block, this can lead to simultaneous writes being triggered on multiple nodes. These simultaneous writes lead to contention and require lock messaging and conversions. By using proper blocks sizes (large blocks aggravate the problem, small ones reduce it) this issue can be mitigated. When using SSD with high bandwidth the duration of transactions, and thus the incidence of simultaneous writes are reduced.

Now that information has been presented on how SSD removes the bandwidth bottleneck for high access files, attention can now be turned to how to locate high concurrent access data files in an Oracle RAC database.

Finding the source of bandwidth bottlenecks

The first step in applying SSD to RAC is to locate the root cause of the I/O contention. The most common cause of I/O bandwidth saturation in Oracle RAC is a poorly performing I/O subsystem. However, more detailed exploration is warranted to see what specific data files contribute to the saturation of the storage. The source of Oracle I/O saturation may be due to one of these causes:

- Non-database processes read from the same device as Oracle data files

- Another database sharing the same file systems (Oracle RAC)

- A poorly tuned I/O subsystem (e.g. RAID5 for high-update data files).

There are two approaches to I/O monitoring Oracle RAC for disk bandwidth bottlenecks:

Monitor enqueues at the disk level – Use OS tools, such as *iostat* of vendor-based disk monitors

Monitor at the Oracle instance level – Use an AWR or STATSPACK report to monitor buffer busy waits and high access times for each instance.

As a review, the hallmark feature of RAC is the ability for many Oracle instances to simultaneously read the Oracle files (Figure 2.6). This complicates the process of locating high concurrent access data files because the file I/O on each of the RAC instances must be interrogated.

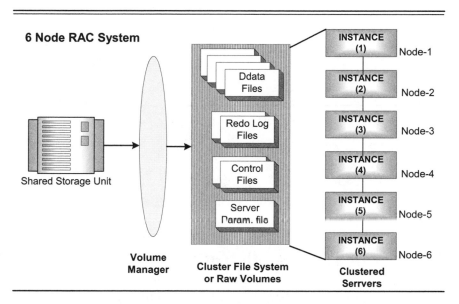

Figure 2.6: *Oracle RAC monitors I/O at the instance level*

Because Oracle file I/O is measured at the instance level, finding bandwidth bottlenecks may mean reading AWR reports on dozens of RAC nodes. To simplify the process of identification, most Oracle professionals will measure I/O at the disk level using native I/O monitors such as *SAR* and *iostat*. They would then look for disk enqueues, a condition where read/write requests are waiting for access to the disk.

In the example below, a SAR command was issued to locate the disk enqueues:

```
root > sar -d -f /var/adm/sa/sa16
```

In the SAR output, review the *avque* column seeking high device backlogs:

```
SunOS prod1 5.6 Generic_105181-23 sun4u     05/16/01

01:00:00 device        %busy   avque   r+w/s  blks/s  avwait  avserv
           sd22          100    72.4    2100    2971     0.0    87.0
           sd23            0     0.0       0       0     0.0     0.0
           sd24            0     0.0       0       0     0.0     0.0
           sd25          100    72.4    2100    2971     0.0    87.0
```

Because of the transient nature of disk enqueues, many Oracle professionals also use disk vendor specific time-series tools (e.g. the *EMC Symmetrics* console) to track disk enqueues over time.

Another approach to locating bandwidth bottlenecks in Oracle RAC is to interrogate each instance for buffer busy waits. The next section examines this closer.

Oracle and Bandwidth Saturation

A sub-optimal disk configuration can make even a well-tuned Oracle RAC database slow to a crawl. An Oracle clustered environment has multiple database instances all sharing the same set of data files. MetaLink Note: 62172.1 notes that the top remedy for increasing DBWR throughput is increasing the speed of the device.

This example from an AWR report from $ORACLE_HOME/rdbms/admin/awrrpt.sql shows an I/O bound database:

```
Top 5 Timed Events
~~~~~~~~~~~~~~~~~                                    % Total
Event                        Waits     Time (s)    Ela Time
--------------------------  ---------  ----------  --------
db file sequential read         2,598       7,146     48.54
db file scattered read         25,519       3,246     22.04
library cache load lock           673       1,363      9.26
CPU time                                    1,154      7.83
log file parallel write        19,157         837      5.68
```

Since most DBAs are too busy to run disk performance scripts on every node of a large RAC cluster, they can look to the web for examples of scripts. Another source is Mike Ault's book *Oracle Disk I/O Tuning* (2004, Rampant TechPress), which also provides a plethora of scripts and examples.

For the vast majority of non-scientific systems, the primary bottleneck is disk I/O. Back in the days before RAID and giant *db_cache_size*, the DBA had to manually load balance the disk I/O sub-system to relieve contention on the disks and the disk controllers. The next section explores this topic.

Examining Real-time disk Statistics

The following scripts can be run anytime against the dynamic *v$* performance views to get a summary of instance-wide activity for a database. By viewing I/O statistics at the tablespace and datafile levels, overworked physical disks can be identified. Should a particular disk or set of disks be under too much strain, the tablespaces can be relocated to less-used devices or new tablespaces can be created on different disks where the hot objects can be moved.

If standard DBA practice has been followed and the indexes have been placed in their own tablespace, the I/O statistics for that tablespace can be viewed to see if the indexes are actually being used

The first step in unraveling any I/O puzzles in databases is to make a quick check of some of the global database I/O metrics. A query such as the *globiostats_rac.sql* script can be used to get a bird's eye view of a database's I/O:

🖫 globiostats_rac.sql

```
-- ***************************************************
-- Copyright © 2005 by Rampant TechPress
-- This script is free for non-commercial purposes
-- with no warranties.  Use at your own risk.
--
-- To license this script for a commercial purpose,
-- contact info@rampant.cc
-- ***************************************************
column sum_io1 new_value st1 noprint
column sum_io2 new_value st2 noprint
column sum_io new_value divide_by noprint
column Percent format 999.999 heading 'Percent|Of IO'
column brratio format 999.99 heading 'Block|Read|Ratio'
column bwratio format 999.99 heading 'Block|Write|Ratio'
column phyrds heading 'Physical | Reads'
column phywrts heading 'Physical | Writes'
column phyblkrd heading 'Physical|Block|Reads'
column phyblkwrt heading 'Physical|Block|Writes'
column name format a45 heading 'File|Name'
column file# format 9999 heading 'File'
column dt new_value today noprint
select to_char(sysdate,'ddmonyyyyhh24miss') dt from dual;
set feedback off verify off lines 132 pages 60 sqlbl on trims on
rem
select
    nvl(sum(a.phyrds+a.phywrts),0) sum_io1
from
    sys.gv_$filestat a;
select nvl(sum(b.phyrds+b.phywrts),0) sum_io2
from
        sys.gv_$tempstat b;
select &st1+&st2 sum_io from dual;
rem
ttitle 'RAC File IO Statistics Report'
spool rac_fileio&&today
select
    a.inst_id, a.file#,b.name, a.phyrds, a.phywrts,
    (100*(a.phyrds+a.phywrts)/&divide_by) Percent,
    a.phyblkrd, a.phyblkwrt, (a.phyblkrd/greatest(a.phyrds,1))
brratio,
     (a.phyblkwrt/greatest(a.phywrts,1)) bwratio
```

```
from
    sys.gv_$filestat a, sys.gv_$dbfile b
where
    a.inst_id=b.inst_id and
    a.file#=b.file#
union
select
    c.inst_id,c.file#,d.name, c.phyrds, c.phywrts,
    (100*(c.phyrds+c.phywrts)/&divide_by) Percent,
    c.phyblkrd, c.phyblkwrt,(c.phyblkrd/greatest(c.phyrds,1))
brratio,
    (c.phyblkwrt/greatest(c.phywrts,1)) bwratio
from
    sys.gv_$tempstat c, sys.gv_$tempfile d
where
        c.inst_id=d.inst_id and
    c.file#=d.file#
order by
    1,2
/
spool off
pause Press enter to continue
set feedback on verify on lines 80 pages 22
clear columns
ttitle off
```

The script queries the *gv$filestat* and *gv$tempstat* views and output from the query might look like the following:

```
Date: 07/08/04                                                            Page:    1
Time: 08:19 AM              File IO Statistics Report                      SYSTEM
                               test database

                                                    Phys Phys  Block Block
           File                    Phys  Phy   Perc. Block Block Read  Write
Inst File  Name                    Reads Writes Of IO Reads Writes Ratio Ratio
---- ----  ------------------------------- ----- ------ ------ ----- ------ ----- -----
   1    1  /U001/oradata/test/system01.dbf   823    96 2.302  1497    96 1.82  1.00
   1    2  /U001/oradata/test/undotbs01.dbf   24   801 2.066    24   801 1.00  1.00
   1   11  /U001/oradata/test/cdfs2_dat01.dbf 13     2  .038    13     2 1.00  1.00
   1   12  /U001/oradata/test/cdfs2_idx01.dbf 866    1 2.171   866     1 1.00  1.00
   2    1  /U001/oradata/test/system01.dbf   293    31  .811   384    31 1.31  1.00
   2    5  /U001/oradata/test/undotbs02.dbf   21   365  .967    21   365 1.00  1.00
   2   12  /U001/oradata/test/cdfs2_idx01.dbf 472    0 1.182   472     0 1.00   .00
   3    1  /U001/oradata/test/system01.dbf   357    33  .977   523    33 1.46  1.00
   3    6  /U001/oradata/test/undotbs03.dbf   25   394 1.049    25   394 1.00  1.00
   3   11  /U002/oradata/test/cdfs2_dat01.dbf 12    38  .125    12    38 1.00  1.00
   4    1  /U001/oradata/test/system01.dbf   163    33  .491   200    33 1.23  1.00
   4    7  /U001/oradata/test/undotbs04.dbf   22   369  .979    22   369 1.00  1.00
   5    1  /U001/oradata/test/system01.dbf   493    30 1.310  1633    30 3.31  1.00
   5    8  /U001/oradata/test/undotbs05.dbf   22   372  .987    22   372 1.00  1.00
   5   11  /U002/oradata/test/cdfs2_dat01.dbf 1027 1138 5.422 16081  1138 15.66 1.00
   6    1  /U001/oradata/test/system01.dbf   238    58  .741   480    58 2.02  1.00
   6    9  /U001/oradata/test/undotbs06.dbf 4281 10821 37.822  4281 10821 1.00  1.00
   6   11  /U002/oradata/test/cdfs2_dat01.dbf 4106 7454 28.951 19725  7454 4.80  1.00
   6   12  /U001/oradata/test/cdfs2_idx01.dbf 2053   46 5.257 13426    46 6.54  1.00
```

This report shows the results from all active instances by using the *gv* settings of views.

Of course just seeing the I/O spread is not much help the goal is to see if there are contention issues. To see contention issues for data blocks, the *gv$waitstat* view will need to be queried.

🖫 Rac_contend.sql

```
--  ****************************************************
--  Copyright © 2005 by Rampant TechPress
--  This script is free for non-commercial purposes
--  with no warranties.  Use at your own risk.
--
--  To license this script for a commercial purpose,
--  contact info@rampant.cc
--  ****************************************************

col avg_wait format a10
set verify off feedback off numwidth 10
set pages 58
set lines 79
column dt new_value today noprint
select to_char(sysdate,'ddmonyyyyhh24miss') dt from dual;
col inst_id format 9999 heading 'inst'
ttitle "rac area of contention report"
spool contend_&&today
select inst_id,class,sum(count) total_waits, sum(time) total_time,
to_char(sum(time)/sum(count),'9,999.999') avg_wait
from gv$waitstat where count>0
group by inst_id, class
order by 1,3 desc;
spool off
set verify on feedback on pages 22 lines 80
ttitle off
```

Some example output from the above script is shown below.

```
Date: 11/30/04                                        Page:    1
Time: 04:48 PM          AREA OF CONTENTION REPORT       PERFSTAT
                            dbp database

   INST_ID CLASS                TOTAL_WAITS TOTAL_TIME AVG_WAIT
---------- ------------------- ----------- ---------- ----------
         1 data block                 6869       2339       .341
         1 segment header                1          0       .000
         2 data block                 1224        241       .197
         2 segment header                1          1      1.000
         3 data block                 1886        388       .206
         3 segment header                1          0       .000
         4 data block                 1404        220       .157
         4 undo header                   3          3      1.000
         4 segment header                1          0       .000
```

Data Block waits indicate contention for system resource at the I/O subsystem level. These should also be traceable by looking for I/O related events within the *gv$system_event* table. One issue with the *gv$system_event* table is that it reports what are known as *idle waits* as well as the *true waits* that should concern the DBA. The next script, *rac_sys_events_pct.sql,* tries to filter out the unimportant events so the real issues are not masked.

🖫 rac_sys_events_pct.sql

```
-- ***************************************************
-- Copyright © 2005 by Rampant TechPress
-- This script is free for non-commercial purposes
-- with no warranties.  Use at your own risk.
--
-- To license this script for a commercial purpose,
-- contact info@rampant.cc
-- ***************************************************
col event format a30 heading 'Event Name'
col waits format 999,999,999 heading 'Total|Waits'
col average_wait format 999,999,999 heading 'Average|Waits'
col time_waited format 999,999,999 heading 'Time Waited'
col total_time new_value divide_by noprint
col value new_value val noprint
col percent format 999.990 heading 'Percent|Of|Non-Idle Waits'
col duration new_value millisec noprint
col p_of_total heading 'Percent|of Total|Uptime' format 999.9999
set lines 132 feedback off verify off pages 50
 select to_number(sysdate-startup_time)*86400*1000 duration from
v$instance;
select
sum(time_waited) total_time
from gv$system_event
where total_waits-total_timeouts>0
     and event not like 'SQL*Net%'
     and event not like 'smon%'
     and event not like 'pmon%'
     and event not like 'rdbms%'
        and event not like 'PX%'
        and event not like 'sbt%'
        and event not like '%slave wait%'
        and event not in ('gcs remote message','ges remote message',
                          'virtual circuit status','dispatcher
timer','wakeup time manager') ;
select max(value) value from gv$sysstat where name ='CPU used when
call started';
ttitle 'RAC System Events Percent'
break on report
compute sum of time_waited on report
spool rep_out/&db/rac_sys_events
select    inst_id,
          name event,
          0 waits,
   0 average_wait,
   value time_waited,
   value/(&&divide_by+&&val)*100 Percent,
   value/&&millisec*100 p_of_total
from gv$sysstat
where name ='CPU used when call started'
```

```
union
select inst_id,
       event,
       total_waits-total_timeouts waits,
       time_waited/(total_waits-total_timeouts) average_wait,
       time_waited,
       time_waited/(&&divide_by+&&val)*100 Percent,
       time_waited/&&millisec*100 P_of_total
from gv$system_event
where total_waits-total_timeouts>0
      and event not like 'SQL*Net%'
      and event not like 'smon%'
      and event not like 'pmon%'
      and event not like 'rdbms%'
          and event not like 'PX%'
          and event not like 'sbt%'
          and event not like '%slave wait%'
          and event not in ('gcs remote message','ges remote message',
                            'virtual circuit status','dispatcher
timer','wakeup time manager')
          and time_waited>0
order by inst_id,percent desc
/
spool off
clear columns
ttitle off
clear computes
clear breaks
```

An example output for a RAC system is shown below.

```
Date: 10/25/04                                                    Page:    1
Time: 02:32 PM                 RAC System Events Percent          PERFSTAT
                                    TEST database

                                               Percent   Percent  Percent
                                     Total  Avg           Of Non-Idle of Total
INST Event Name                      Waits Waits Time Waited    Waits   Uptime
---- ------------------------------ ----------- ----- ----------- ----------- --------
   1 enqueue                            241,569  165  39,834,044   17.246  10.0116
   1 lock manager wait for remote m 357,670,752    0  31,566,868   13.667   7.9338
     essage
   1 CPU used when call started               0    0   6,426,632    2.782   1.6152
   1 global cache cr request          35,512,634    0   5,046,167    2.185   1.2683
   1 db file sequential read          14,033,920    0   2,541,747    1.100    .6388
   1 db file scattered read           17,108,576    0   2,459,243    1.065    .6181
   1 latch free                       22,215,925    0   1,013,336     .439    .2547
   1 global cache lock null to x         521,382    2     858,435     .372    .2158
   1 log file sync                     1,772,257    0     356,476     .154    .0896
   1 control file sequential read      5,060,170    0     353,548     .153    .0889
   2 enqueue                             968,097   42  40,205,562   17.407  10.1050
   2 lock manager wait for remote m 241,120,325    0  29,961,451   12.972   7.5303
     essage
   2 CPU used when call started               0    0  23,487,063   10.169   5.9031
   2 global cache cr request         121,835,757    0  19,421,720    8.409   4.8813
   2 db file scattered read           56,823,980    0   9,829,920    4.256   2.4706
   2 latch free                      237,139,741    0   8,293,937    3.591   2.0845
   2 db file sequential read          40,913,992    0   7,630,938    3.304   1.9179
   2 log file sync                     3,784,667    0   1,038,734     .450    .2611
   2 global cache lock busy             516,508    2     793,076     .343    .1993
   2 log file parallel write          3,955,088    0     684,390     .296    .1720
                                                     -----------
sum                                                   237,396,648
```

So in this example report there are many events, but the ones that
are probably causing most of the issues are actually the I/O
related events *db file sequential read* and *db file scattered read*.

The *gv$session_wait* view can also be examined to see how many sessions are impacted by the I/O related problem events.

💾 **check_io_waits_rac.sql**

```
-- ***************************************************
-- Copyright © 2005 by Rampant TechPress
-- This script is free for non-commercial purposes
-- with no warranties.  Use at your own risk.
--
-- To license this script for a commercial purpose,
-- contact info@rampant.cc
-- ***************************************************

select
   inst_id,
   count(*),
   event
from
   gv$session_wait
where
   wait_time != 0
and

   event IN
   ('db file sequential read','db file scattered read')
group by
   inst_id,event
order by 1 desc;
```

Here is a sample of the output from this query:

```
INST_ID  COUNT(*) EVENT
-------  -------- -----------------------------------------------
      1       122 db file sequential reads
      1       100 db file scattered reads
      2       156 db file sequential reads
      2        78 db file scattered reads
```

Another important measurement is the actual timing. It should be noted that on some systems and some disk subsystems the I/O timing data can be bogus. It is a good practice to compare it against actual *iostat* numbers. An example I/O timing report is shown below.

```
FILE# NAME                                PHYRDS  PHYWRTS   READTIM/    WRITETIM/
                                                            PHYRDS      PHYWRTS
----- ----------------------------------- ------- -------- ----------- -----------
    5 /oracle/oradata/testdb/tools01_01.dbf     318      153 .377358491  .150326797
    1 /oracle/oradata/testdb/system01.dbf      3749      806 .332622033  2.3101737
    9 /oracle/oradata/testdb/tcmd_data01_03.dbf 442389   1575 .058064283  6.90095238
    8 /oracle/oradata/testdb/tcmd_data01_02.dbf 540596   2508 .057647485  5.11961722
    7 /oracle/oradata/testdb/tcmd_data01_01.dbf 14446868 1177 .036516842  2.62531861
   10 /oracle/oradata/testdb/tcmd_idx01_02.dbf  15694   5342 .035746145  6.50074878
    3 /oracle/oradata/testdb/rbs01_01.dbf        757   25451 .034346103  10.7960002
   11 /oracle/oradata/testdb/tcmd_data01_04.dbf   1391    606 .023005032  6.66336634
    6 /oracle/oradata/testdb/tcmd_idx01_01.dbf 1148402  10220 .015289942  6.35831703
    2 /oracle/oradata/testdb/temp01_01.dbf     34961    8835    0           0
    4 /oracle/oradata/testdb/users01_01.dbf       78      76    0           0

11 rows selected.
```

The output in the listing above shows that all of the I/O timing is at or below 10 milliseconds. Normally, this would be considered good performance for disks, however, most modern arrays can give sub-millisecond response times by use of caching and by spreading I/O across multiple platters.

While many "experts" say anything less than 10-20 milliseconds is good, that was based on old disk technology. If a disk system is not giving response times that are at 5 milliseconds or less then it may be prudent to look at tuning the I/O subsystems.

Another interesting statistic is the overall I/O rate for the system as it relates to Oracle. This is easily calculated using PL/SQL as is shown below.

🖫 get_io_rac.sql

```
--  ***************************************************
--  Copyright © 2003 by Rampant TechPress
--  This script is free for non-commercial purposes
--  with no warranties.  Use at your own risk.
--
--  To license this script for a commercial purpose,
--  contact info@rampant.cc
--  ***************************************************

set serveroutput on
declare
cursor get_io is select
        nvl(sum(a.phyrds+a.phywrts),0)  sum_io1,to_number(null)
sum_io2
from sys.gv_$filestat a
union
```

```
select
        to_number(null) sum_io1, nvl(sum(b.phyrds+b.phywrts),0)
sum_io2
from
        sys.gv_$tempstat b;
now date;
elapsed_seconds number;
sum_io1 number;
sum_io2 number;
sum_io12 number;
sum_io22 number;
tot_io number;
tot_io_per_sec number;
fixed_io_per_sec number;
temp_io_per_sec number;
begin
open get_io;
for i in 1..2 loop
fetch get_io into sum_io1, sum_io2;
if i = 1 then sum_io12:=sum_io1;
else
sum_io22:=sum_io2;
end if;
end loop;

select sum_io12+sum_io22 into tot_io from dual;
select sysdate into now from dual;
select ceil((now-max(startup_time))*(60*60*24)) into elapsed_seconds
from gv$instance;
fixed_io_per_sec:=sum_io12/elapsed_seconds;
temp_io_per_sec:=sum_io22/elapsed_seconds;
tot_io_per_sec:=tot_io/elapsed_seconds;
dbms_output.put_line('Elapsed Sec :'||to_char(elapsed_seconds,
'9,999,999.99'));
dbms_output.put_line('Fixed
IO/SEC:'||to_char(fixed_io_per_sec,'9,999,999.99'));
dbms_output.put_line('Temp IO/SEC :'||to_char(temp_io_per_sec,
'9,999,999.99'));
dbms_output.put_line('Total IO/SEC:'||to_char(tot_io_Per_Sec,
'9,999,999.99'));
end;
/
```

An example of the output from this report is shown below.

```
SQL> @io_sec

Elapsed Sec :    43,492.00
Fixed IO/SEC:       588.33
Temp IO/SEC :        95.01
Total IO/SEC:       683.34

PL/SQL procedure successfully executed
```

By examining the total average IO/SEC for the database, it is possible to determine if the I/O subsystem is capable of handling the load. In this case at least 5-6 disks will be needed to handle the IO load. The Oracle Automatic Session History (ASH) tables can also be used to locate "hot" data files and tables.

Locating Slow Disk with ASH

A snapshot of Oracle wait events can be obtained every hour with the Oracle 10g Automatic Session History (ASH) tables. This information can be used to plot changes in wait behavior over time. Thresholds can also be set so that reporting is done only on wait events that exceed those pre-defined thresholds. Here is the script that is commonly used for exception reporting of wait events.

🖫 ash_event_rollup.sql

```
-- *****************************************************
-- Copyright © 2003 by Rampant TechPress
-- This script is free for non-commercial purposes
-- with no warranties.  Use at your own risk.
--
-- To license this script for a commercial purpose,
-- contact info@rampant.cc
-- *****************************************************

ttitle 'High waits on events|Rollup by hour'


column mydate heading 'Yr.  Mo Dy Hr'      format a13;
column event                               format a30;
column total_waits     heading 'tot waits' format 999,999;
column time_waited     heading 'time wait' format 999,999;
column total_timeouts heading 'timeouts'  format 9,999;
break on to_char(snap_time,'yyyy-mm-dd') skip 1;

 select
   to_char(e.sample_time,'yyyy-mm-dd HH24')   mydate,
   e.event,
   count(e.event)                            total_waits,
   sum(e.time_waited)                        time_waited
from
   v$active_session_history e
where
   e.event not like '%timer'
and
   e.event not like '%message%'
and
   e.event not like '%slave wait%'
having
   count(e.event) > 100
group by
   to_char(e.sample_time,'yyyy-mm-dd HH24'),
   e.event
```

```
order by 1
;
```

The output from this script is show below. A time-series report is the result, showing those days and hours when the thresholds are exceeded. Notice where every evening between 10:00 PM and 11:00 PM high I/O waits on the Oracle redo logs are being experienced.

```
Wed Aug 21                                                page    1
                        High waits on events
                          Rollup by hour

Yr.  Mo Dy Hr EVENT                              tot waits time wait
------------- ------------------------------     --------- ---------
2002-08-18 22 LGWR wait for redo copy                9,326     1,109
2002-08-18 23 LGWR wait for redo copy                8,506       316
2002-08-18 23 buffer busy waits                        214    21,388
2002-08-19 00 LGWR wait for redo copy                  498         5
2002-08-19 01 LGWR wait for redo copy                  497        15
2002-08-19 22 LGWR wait for redo copy                9,207     1,433
2002-08-19 22 buffer busy waits                        529    53,412
2002-08-19 23 LGWR wait for redo copy                9,066       367
2002-08-19 23 buffer busy waits                        250    24,479
2002-08-20 00 LGWR wait for redo copy                  771        16
2002-08-20 22 LGWR wait for redo copy                8,030     2,013
2002-08-20 22 buffer busy waits                        356    35,583
2002-08-20 23 LGWR wait for redo copy                8,021       579
2002-08-20 23 buffer busy waits                        441    44,677
2002-08-21 00 LGWR wait for redo copy                1,013        26
2002-08-21 00 rdbms ipc reply                          160    30,986
2002-08-21 01 LGWR wait for redo copy                  541        17
```

AWR can also be used to drill-down and see the specific tables and indexes that are experiencing slow I/O. The following *wait_time_detail.sql* script compares the wait event values from *dba_hist_waitstat* and *dba_hist_active_sess_history*. The exact objects that are experiencing wait events can be identified.

🖫 wait_time_detail.sql

```
set pages 999
set lines 80

break on snap_time skip 2

col snap_time      heading 'Snap|Time'    format a20
col file_name      heading 'File|Name'    format a40
col object_type    heading 'Object|Type'  format a10
col object_name    heading 'Object|Name'  format a20
col wait_count     heading 'Wait|Count'   format 999,999
col time           heading 'Time'         format 999,999

select
   to_char(begin_interval_time,'yyyy-mm-dd hh24:mi') snap_time,
--   file_name,
   object_type,
   object_name,
   wait_count,
   time
from
   dba_hist_waitstat            wait,
   dba_hist_snapshot            snap,
   dba_hist_active_sess_history ash,
   dba_data_files               df,
   dba_objects                  obj
where
   wait.snap_id = snap.snap_id
and
   wait.snap_id = ash.snap_id
and
   df.file_id = ash.current_file#
and
   obj.object_id = ash.current_obj#
and
   wait_count > 50
order by
   to_char(begin_interval_time,'yyyy-mm-dd hh24:mi'),
   file_name;
```

Note that this script is enabled to join into the *dba_data_files* view to get the file names associated with the wait event. This is a very powerful script that can be used to quickly drill-in to find the cause of specific waits. Below is sample output.

```
SQL> @wait_time_detail


This will compare values from dba_hist_waitstat with
detail information from dba_hist_active_sess_history.


Snap                  Object     Object              Wait
Time                  Type       Name                Count      Time
--------------------  ---------  ------------------  --------   --------
2004-02-28 01:00      TABLE      ORDOR                4,273          67
                      INDEX      PK_CUST_ID          12,373         324
                      INDEX      FK_CUST_NAME         3,883          17
                      INDEX      PK_ITEM_ID           1,256         967
```

```
2004-02-29 03:00     TABLE      ITEM_DETAIL      83        69

2004-03-01 04:00     TABLE      ITEM_DETAIL    1,246       45

2004-03-01 21:00     TABLE      CUSTOMER_DET   4,381      354
                     TABLE      IND_PART         117       15

2004-03-04 01:00     TABLE      MARVIN        41,273       16
                     TABLE      FACTOTUM       2,827       43
                     TABLE      DOW_KNOB         853        6
                     TABLE      ITEM_DETAIL       57      331
                     TABLE      HIST_ORD       4,337      176
                     TABLE      TAB_HIST         127       66
```

RAC I/O bandwidth issues

In general, Oracle RAC systems with bandwidth saturation may manifest high *buffer busy waits* and *write complete waits*. Sometimes *enqueue* and *db file parallel writes* may also be seen. For example:

```
                                 Total      Wait      wait    Waits   Avg
                                                                      Event
Wait                             Waits    Timeouts  Time (cs)  (ms)   /txn
------------------------------ ----------- --------- --------- ----- ------
buffer busy waits                225,559   211,961  24,377,029  1081   4.0
enqueue                           25,731    21,756   6,786,722  2638   0.5
Parallel Query Idle Wait - S       9,980     7,929   1,762,606  1766   0.2
SQL*Net message from dblink      435,845         0   1,288,965    30   7.7
db file parallel write             4,252         0   1,287,023  3027   0.1
write complete waits               5,872     5,658     581,066   990   0.1
db file sequential read        1,249,981         0     510,793     4  22.0
```

If there are write-based disk bandwidth issues, the Oracle database writer (DBWR) process might show slow performance in the form of:

- Low number of DBWR Timeouts

- Higher than average "dirty buffers inspected"

- The ratio of "free buffers inspected" to "free buffers requested" exceeds 5%

```
Statistic                       Total    per Second   per Trans
----------------------------- --------- ------------ -----------
consistent changes               43,523      12.1         2.4
free buffer inspected             6,087       1.7         0.3
free buffer requested           416,010     115.6        23.1
logons cumulative                15,718       4.4         0.9
physical writes                  24,757       6.9         1.4
write requests                      634       0.2         0.0
```

While buffer busy waits are most commonly associated with segment header contention onside the data buffer pool (*db_cache_size*, etc.), buffer busy waits are also caused by disk I/O issues.

MetaLink note: 155971.1 suggests that buffer-busy waits can signal I/O bandwidth saturation:

> The cause for the buffer busy waits and other related waits might be a saturated disk controller or subsystem impacting the database's ability to read or write blocks. The disk/controller may be saturated because of the many core dumps occurring simultaneously requiring hundreds of megabytes each.

When there is disk controller contention causing *buffer busy waits*, one approach is to move the offending data files to a device with greater bandwidth.

Conclusion

Because of the architecture of Oracle Real Application Clusters where many computers access a shared set of data files, disk related I/O bandwidth problems are epidemic.

The intelligent replacement of disks with SSD for high concurrent access data files can result in stunning performance improvements. The main points of this chapter include:

- The vast majority of RAC performance problems relate to disk I/O bottlenecks that are caused by the inherent limited bandwidth of platter-based data storage.

- The architecture of SSD allows super-high concurrent access to high-impact Oracle data files.

- Removing the disk bottlenecks in a RAC environment removes disk saturation and allows Oracle to make more efficient use of CPU resources.

- High concurrent access data files can be identified with OS and disk utilities, seeking disk enqueues.

- Within Oracle, I/O waits can be tracked at the data file, tablespace and table level using Oracle's AWR and ASH tables.

The next chapter explores the uses of solid state drives with Oracle10g RAC and how to use Oracle statistics to determine where best to utilize SSD technology.

Solid-State Disk with RAC

I told them we needed a faster interconnect!

Introduction

Oracle Real Application Clusters (RAC) is a virtualized memory system that depends on a high speed interconnect to provide a single memory image across multiple host machines. This concept is illustrated in Figure 3.1.

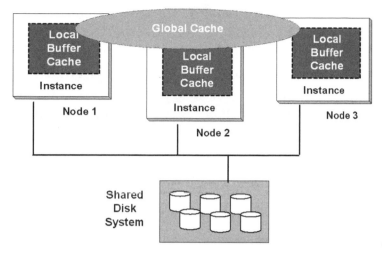

Figure 3.1: *Virtualization of Memory in RAC*

Performance in a RAC environment is generally maximized when a majority of data is cached within the virtualized memory area. Once a database is fully cached, the performance of the system then becomes dependent upon the speed of the memory-to-memory transfers via the interconnect. As a result, the overall performance of the entire system will be dependent on the speed and latency of the cluster interconnect protocol.

When the system is not fully cached, performance becomes codependent on the underlying disk I/O subsystem and the interconnect with a convoy effect. The convoy effect is a term used to describe how a set of dependent objects such as ships, cars, or computers becomes limited by the speed of the slowest member. In most computer systems where there is an interconnect and disks, the disks are the slowest performers. Therefore, the speed at which an I/O subsystem can service requests depends ultimately on the latency of the systems disks, even when masked with memory caches.

The I/O subsystem consists of device types which map to drivers. In turn, the drivers send the requests for I/O to a host bus adapter (HBA). The HBA converts the request to the proper format for the protocol being used, such as fibre, copper, or other protocols. The request is then transferred over that protocol to the storage subsystem I/O bus to the storage controller, depending on whether the request can be satisfied via a cache read or must be read from disk the controller either reads from cache or disk. A typical subsystem is shown in Figure 3.2.

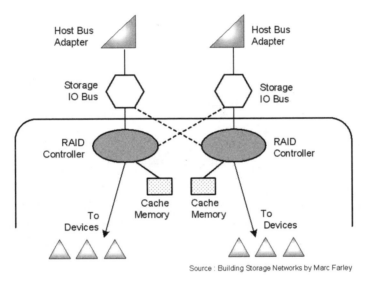

Source : Building Storage Networks by Marc Farley

Figure 3.2: *Typical Disk IO Subsystem*

Of course the disk I/O subsystem also allows virtualization of the true underlying disk structures as shown in Figure 3.3. All of this I/O subsystem and disk activity can exact an extreme penalty on Oracle and Oracle RAC performance if any piece of the underlying structure is improperly configured.

Possible configuration issues include the SCSI interface, the proper use of disk managers, proper application of striping technology, proper stripe width and depths and the list goes on and on. Many times the system administrator and DBA throw up their hands and just accept whatever the vendor does to setup the disks and I/O subsystem. This often leads to sub-optimal performance.

An example of a disk array parameter that directly impacts performance is disk stripe width. For the purpose of this text, disk stripe width defined to mean the amount of a stripe in a RAID configuration that resides on one disk. In early systems, the advice of many experts was to stripe shallow and wide. For example, one might use an 8k stripe width across 32 drives. This was based on rapidly retrieving a single large file. However, Oracle usually retrieves small reads such as single data values after index lookups. It does hundreds, if not thousands, of these in a single second in large systems. This means Oracle disk arrays must be tuned for concurrency. In Oracle systems, a stripe width that is too narrow is guaranteed to generate I/O contention. Oracle recommends a stripe width of between 128K (non-data) to 1 megabyte (data).

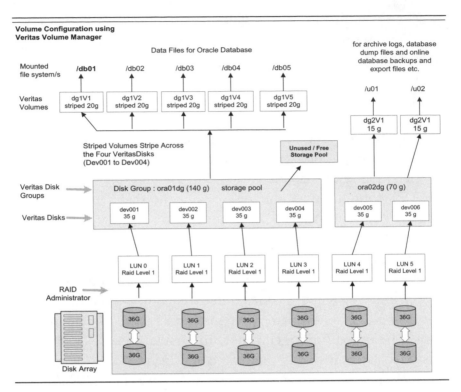

Figure 3.3: *Example Disk Virtualizations*

With any physical device that depends on the mechanical motion of actuator arms and spinning disks, there is also the issue of disk arm positional latency and disk rotational latency. They severely limit the effective speed of I/O for physical disks. Generally, non-linear I/O rates are only in the tens to hundreds of megabits per second. Many disk array manufacturers are getting around this through the implementation of huge memory caches, so not only do users get to pay for the disks, they get to pay for the memory caches as well. With disks running anywhere from $500-$3000 US, depending on the vendor from which they are acquired and what firmware has been loaded onto them, paying for both seems a bit redundant. In an SSD environment, the disks are there strictly as a backing store, since no large I/O rate is needed for this, there is no need to buy five or ten disks to get the I/O needed. Just one can cover several units; although for redundancy, the backing store is usually mirrored.

Solid-state disk (SSD) technology is replacing ancient spinning platters of magnetic coated media with an array of super fast solid-state RAM. Today's SSD devices achieve tertiary storage with software mechanisms that write the RAM frames to a back end disk on the device.

With the cost of SSD at only $1k/gig, many Oracle systems administrators are exploring how to leverage this powerful performance tool for their environment. Smaller databases can now run fully cached with SSD, yet there is a debate about the proper use of SSD in an Oracle environment. Should it be used for redo? How about undo segments? Maybe temp? This debate becomes even more muddled with real application clusters (RAC) thrown into the picture.

With a standard Oracle database, the SSD array, when not used for the entire database, is best used for the files where the most I/O contention exists. For example, in an online transaction system indexes, redo, or temp may be best placed on SSD, while in a decision support or warehouse, temp and data files may be the best choice.

As this study has determined, RAC files placed on SSD may differ completely from those that might be considered in a non-RAC environment.

Use of SSD With RAC

Guess I should have put that file on SSD!

Where does SSD technology fit into the RAC environment? Of course if allowed, replacement of the entire disk subsystem would provide the maximum amount of performance gain, but what if the entire disk setup cannot be replaced?

With a RAC environment, the largest performance boost will come with placing the files with blocks that are either most read from disk, or are most passed across the interconnect, on SSD arrays.

For example, the results of block transfer across an interconnect will look like the following:

```
Segments by CR Blocks Received

                                                     CR
          Tablespace                   Subobject Obj.  Blocks
Owner     Name       Object Name       Name      Type  Received %Total
------    ---------- ----------------- --------- ----- -------- ------
TPCC      USERS      C_ORDER                     TABLE   36,613  40.59
TPCC      USERS      C_STOCK                     TABLE   17,938  19.89
TPCC      USERS      C_ORDER_LINE_I1             INDEX   10,485  11.62
TPCC      USERS      C_DISTRICT                  TABLE    6,834   7.58
TPCC      USERS      C_NEW_ORDER_I1              INDEX    6,256   6.94
          -----------------------------------------------------------
```

```
Segments by Current Blocks Received

                                                          Current
          Tablespace                    Subobject  Obj.   Blocks
Owner     Name        Object Name       Name       Type   Received  %Total
------    ----------  ----------------  ---------  -----  --------- ------
TPCC      USERS       C_ORDER                      TABLE    181,196  77.75
TPCC      USERS       C_STOCK                      TABLE     15,017   6.44
TPCC      USERS       C_NEW_ORDER_I1               INDEX      7,149   3.07
TPCC      USERS       C_DISTRICT                   TABLE      6,781   2.91
TPCC      USERS       C_ORDER_LINE_I1              INDEX      4,446   1.91
          ---------------------------------------------------------- -----
```

In this example, the *c_order*, *c_district* and *c_stock* tables and the *c_order_line_i1* and *c_new_order_i1* indexes are the best candidates to be moved to SSD, assuming memory modifications are done to ensure they are read from disk.

Oracle Corporation states that index blocks are the most frequently shipped blocks across an interconnect. By placing the indexes in a specialized different block size area of the *db buffer caches* and then sizing that to hold a minimal amount of blocks, the index blocks can be forced to be read from an SSD drive. The TPC-C tests in Chapter 4 show that for RAC on SSD, forcing the system to read the blocks rather than transferring them through the interconnect, is the best performance methodology.

The Balancing Act

In order to determine the best utilization of SSD resources, the DBA must completely understand the various latencies in their system. RAC related latencies fall under two broad categories:

- Interconnect latencies

- Disk I/O related latencies

Interconnect latencies are calculated based on the Oracle internal views. Contention in blocks can be measured using the block transfer time. To determine block transfer time, the statistics *gc cr block receive time* and *gc cr blocks received* should be examined. The

---

time is determined by calculating the ratio of *gc cr block receive time* to *gc cr blocks received*. The following script shows this calculation.

```
column "AVG RECEIVE TIME (ms)" format 9999999.9
col inst_id for 9999
prompt GCS CR BLOCKS
select b1.inst_id, b2.value "RECEIVED",
b1.value "RECEIVE TIME",
((b1.value / b2.value) * 10) "AVG RECEIVE TIME (ms)"
from gv$sysstat b1, gv$sysstat b2
where b1.name = 'gc cr block receive time' and
b2.name = 'gc cr blocks received' and b1.inst_id = b2.inst_id
```

An example from the actual system on which the TPC-C tests were performed is shown below.

```
INST_ID   RECEIVED RECEIVE TIME AVG RECEIVE TIME (ms)
-------   -------- ------------ ---------------------
      2      86867        16663                   1.9
      1      85555        17148                   2.0
```

In this example, it is taking nearly two milliseconds to transfer blocks from one RAC node to another. The average read time for a block from SSD by Oracle10g was between 0.091 and .000 milliseconds:

```
Date: 07/29/05                                            Page:    1
Time: 06:51 AM            IO Timing Analysis                   TPCC
                             ssd database
           File                              PHY  PHY  PHY  PHY
Inst File  Name                              RDS WRTS RDTM WRTM
---- ----  ---------------------------------- ------ ----- ---- ----
   2    1  UNDOTBS1 /oracle2/oradata/ssd/temp01.dbf        11      0 .091 .000
   1    4  USERS /oracle2/oradata/ssd/ssd_data01.dbf   189357  84285 .032 .014
   2    1  UNDOTBS1 /oracle2/oradata/ssd/system01.dbf     2835     82 .031 .000
   2    4  USERS /oracle2/oradata/ssd/ssd_data01.dbf   162718  66945 .029 .014
   2    3  TEMP /oracle2/oradata/ssd/sysaux01.dbf        681    306 .025 .016
   1    2  SYSAUX /oracle2/oradata/ssd/undotbs01.dbf      609   4972 .021 .021
   1    1  UNDOTBS1 /oracle2/oradata/ssd/system01.dbf     3434    190 .018 .005
   1    3  TEMP /oracle2/oradata/ssd/sysaux01.dbf        490    169 .016 .006
   2    2  SYSAUX /oracle2/oradata/ssd/undotbs01.dbf      148      8 .014 .125
   2    5  UNDOTBS2 /oracle2/oradata/ssd/undotbs02.dbf     524   4147 .013 .020
   1    1  UNDOTBS1 /oracle2/oradata/ssd/temp01.dbf         9      0 .000 .000
   1    5  UNDOTBS2 /oracle2/oradata/ssd/undotbs02.dbf       6      4 .000 .000
```

From these results, it is clear that one will get a factor of 100-200 increase in speed by reading the blocks from SSD rather than across this particular interconnect. Of course, many interconnects can beat this type of transfer speed, so results may vary. The results shown above are from the actual SSD testing and reflect up to a 600 user load on the system. The typical latencies for various interconnect technologies are shown in Table 3.1.

MEASUREMENT	SMP BUS	MEMORY CHANNEL	MYRINET	SUN SCI	GIG ENET
Latency (uS)	0.5	3	7 to 9	10	100
CPU Overhead	<1	<1	<1		~100
Msg/Sec(million)	>10	>2			<0.1
Bandwidth MB/s	>500	>100	~250	~70	~50

Table 3.1: *Typical Network Latencies*

The statistics in Table 3.1 can be misleading. The latency must be measured inside the Oracle system not just at the network. Oracle internal messaging, latching, and locking all add to the Oracle latency as reported in previous results. The reported latency over the gigabyte Ethernet is 100 *u*S, yet ten times that, 1.9 to 2.0 milliseconds, is seen as the block transfer latency.

Obviously, in the above system, moving the reading of blocks to SSD makes sense. In most systems, the same I/O timings for a RAID disk array will range from one to two milliseconds to over 20 depending on how full the disk is and how many users need access to the same disks at the same time. The output below shows a typical response profile for a RAID based fibre channel array.

```
Date: 08/12/05                                                    Page:
1
Time:  10:40  AM                              IO   Timing   Analysis
PERFSTAT
                           atltest database


                                    Phys.  Phys. Avg.Read Avg.Write
File# Name                          Reads  Wrts      Time      Time
----- ------------------------------ ------ ----- -------- ---------
   29 /u03/oradata/atltest/eebase_dm.dbf    3945   2824 1.318377 149.03718
    1 /u02/oradata/atltest/temp.dbf        38590  25594 1.301528  86.38509
    1 /u01/oradata/atltest/system01.dbf     6234   5122  .827879 137.78680
   30 /u03/oradata/atltest/eebase_dl.dbf   14513   1955  .716461  59.00716
   31 /u03/oradata/atltest/eebase_is.dbf     176   4365  .636363 434.92348
```

```
 5 /u01/oradata/atltest/BFAPP_STATIC_D.dbf      927     283  .633225    4.59717
19 /u01/oradata/atltest/BFLOB_D.dbf            4874    5690  .615510    3.00615
 7 /u01/oradata/atltest/BFAUD_OBJECTS_D.dbf     599     238  .525876    2.75210
 3 /u01/oradata/atltest/BFAPP_D.dbf            9582     688  .494051   10.68313
35 /u03/oradata/atltest/eeaudit_im.dbf         4852   29644  .481038  132.40284
 9 /u01/oradata/atltest/BFAUD_STATIC_D.dbf      682     232  .439882    2.53879
 4 /u02/oradata/atltest/BFAPP_I.dbf            1077     648  .436397    5.00925
13 /u01/oradata/atltest/BFEDI_D.dbf            7630     174  .432110    9.10344
28 /u03/oradata/atltest/3x_is.dbf              186   13953  .419354  271.65455
22 /u02/oradata/atltest/indx01.dbf             382    2230  .403141   49.80896
11 /u02/oradata/atltest/BFAUDIT_D.dbf        49326    1743  .393017  130.45438
17 /u01/oradata/atltest/BFERROR_D.dbf        11401    1577  .392684  145.88839
24 /u01/oradata/atltest/tools01.dbf            358     302  .388268   27.23841
14 /u02/oradata/atltest/BFEDI_I.dbf            299     247  .344481    4.83400
 6 /u02/oradata/atltest/BFAPP_STATIC_I.dbf     431     312  .338747    5.54807
```

For a RAID type array, the interconnect performs faster, so best performance comes from fully caching the database.

One additional issue with disks versus SSD technology deals with how the amount of data stored on a disk affects performance. As the amount of data on a single disk increases, the performance of that disk will decrease. This is due to the increased positioning and rotational latencies required as the storage of information moves away from the outer and middle cylinders towards the inner cylinders on the drive. Back in the old days, system administrators spent hours repositioning files into the sweet spots of disk performance and away from the dead zone. Now with automated load balancing and RAID, system administrators have little real control over file placement. Experts agree that for optimal performance, no disk should be filled to more than 60% of its total capacity, which is rather like buying a six passenger car and being told that it only four people should be transported in it.

Also, no matter how fast the disk spins, it can still only service a single read per operation. Now, modern disk controllers may optimize these single reads into a series of reads, but the heads can only be in one position at a time. This requires consideration of the I/O per second needed for the disk array with this sometimes overshadowing disk size as the predominant consideration in buying an array. For example, a 100 gigabyte database will entirely fit on a single 148 GB disk drive; however, at least 500-1000 I/O's per second will be required to satisfy user demands depending on transactions per minute and transaction size. To satisfy 500-1000 I/O's per second, five to ten disk drives would be required.

On SSD technology, the complete capacity is usable since there is no positional or rotational latency, and the number of simultaneous reads/writes is only dependent on bandwidth since there is no head that needs to be repositioned after each read or write operation. For the 100 GB database in the above example, 100 GBs of SSD storage would likely be purchased.

Disk latencies are often quoted at around four to seven milliseconds on most modern hardware. With arrays with large caches, the read times can be reduced to near SSD values. Of course, this approach of placing large caches in front of the disk array is essentially using solid-state technology with the disks as a backing store, so better performance would be an expectation. The main problem with most disk arrays with large caches is that the caches are usually limited to about 32 GBs, and again, for the cost includes a memory cache as well as expensive disks.

Conclusion

This chapter has shown situations in which it would be best to employ solid state disk technology in an Oracle10g RAC environment. The best performance, of course, comes from replacing the entire disk I/O subsystem with SSD technology. However, that course of action may not be doable in every environment. In that case, the system should be analyzed to determine what blocks are being shipped the most across the interconnect or are being read from existing disk technology. The solution would be to create a new tablespace with a different block size and a data block cache area to support it. The data block cache area should be sized small enough to force reads from the SSD to satisfy the user's requests. At that point, the objects can be moved into the new tablespace.

In the next chapter the actual TPC-C benchmarks showing how SSD compares to SATA arrays will be reviewed. The various memory sizes will also be explored and performance for the two basic configurations that are affected will be examined.

TPC-C Online Benchmark With Solid-State Disk

Get me the DBA! I need a TPC-C Benchmark by Lunch!

In this chapter the results from a TPC-C benchmark using solid-state drives and Oracle10g RAC (real application cluster) technology will be examined. The benchmark shows the effects of varying the SGA buffer size on RAC performance in both a RAID array and solid-state drive configurations.

The purpose of this test was to show the affects of reduction of memory on systems using Oracle10g RAC and both RAID and solid-state disk technologies.

Test Setup:

Using the standard TPC-C protocol, the utilization of Oracle10g Real Application Clusters with both a solid-state array and a fiber channel attached SATA disk array was tested. Using a 16-warehouse configuration for the TPC-C schema produced a 2.4 gigabyte test database when utilizing the transaction-processing template database provided by the Oracle DBCA utility. The database was created with no sample schemas included. Identical databases where used on the RAID and SSD arrays. The entity-relationship diagram and table descriptions for the TPC-C benchmark are shown in Appendix A.

The systems utilized 2 dual AMD 244 processor 1.7 Ghz Opteron servers with a CPU cache size of 1MB running Red Hat Linux EL with kernel 2.4.21-27.ELsmp. Both servers have 2GB of memory. Each server has one dual ported Qlogic 2342 HBA installed. One port connected to the RamSan and one to the RAID array. The array is configured as a RAID 5 with a segment size of 64k (stripe width). The stripe is across 5 disks in a 64 Gigabyte total filesystem size. Each disk is a SATA Maxtor MaxLine Plus II with a capacity of 250GB. The disks have a speed of 7200 RPM and an 8MB cache buffer. Server connection to the array is via 2-Gbit Fibre Channel HBA (QL 2342). The servers are connected to the test desktops via the web. There were four client test desktops of various configurations running Windows XP and Window 2000 utilizing the Benchmark Factory agent software to act as test machines controlled by the main Benchmark test director located on the mralaptop2 test machine. The system utilizes the Gigabit Nextreme NIC for the public network and Oracle VIP and the 82557x Pro Ethernet gigabit adapter for the RAC interconnect. This configuration is shown in Figure 4.1.

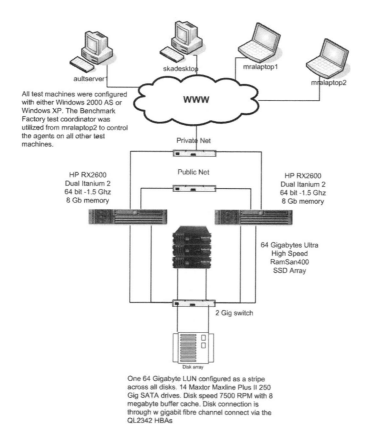

All test machines were configured with either Windows 2000 AS or Windows XP. The Benchmark Factory test coordinator was utilized from mralaptop2 to control the agents on all other test machines.

Figure 4.1: *Test Architecture*

The overall disk specifications are in Table 4.1.

SPEC	VALUE
Speed	7200 RPM
Capacity	250GB
Interface	SATA or PATA
Max sustained data transfer rate	up to 59MB/sec (59 1 meg IO/sec)
Average seek time (latency)	9.0 ms
Max burst transfer speeds	up to 150MB/sec
Cache buffer	8MB

Table 4.1: *MaxLine Plus II Disk Specifications*

The overall RamSan400 Specifications are in Table 4.2.

SPEC	VALUE
Fibre Channels: 4Gb	2 to 8 Ports
I/Os per second	400,000
Power Supplies	3 Redundant
Bandwidth	3 GB/sec
Backup Disk Drives	Redundant Hot-Swap
Capacity	32-128 GB per Unit
Latency	<14 microseconds
Batteries	Redundant Hot-Swap
Size	5.25" (3U) x 25"
Weight (maximum)	80 lbs
Power Consumption (peak)	350 Watts

Table 4.2: *RamSan400 Specifications*

The database schema (Appendix A) was loaded using the Benchmark Factory tool from Quest software. A 16 warehouse configuration, that was approximately 2.4 gigabytes with indexes, required about 6 hours to build. The schema was then exported and subsequent reloads were performed using the export. The Benchmark Factory was also utilized to perform the TPC-C transaction runs and load generations from 10 to 600 users. The default weighting for transactions, which matches that specified in the TPC-C benchmark specification, was utilized. Figure 4.2 shows the main screen from the Benchmark Factory Application.

The use of the Benchmark Factory tool allowed multiple runs of the benchmark without having to perform programming. Essentially the steps performed were:

1. Set up the number of warehouses required. This is determined empirically to achieve the proper database size.

2. Build the database schema and load data

3. Export the database to use for reloading. The build part of the tool requires several hours to build a database so this step is critical.

4. Run the benchmarks

5. Drop and Reload the database.

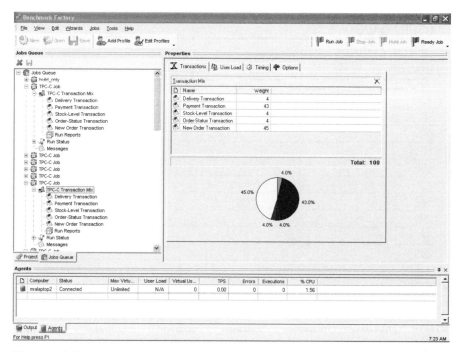

Figure 4.2: *Benchmark Factory Main Screen*

Table 4.3 shows the typical transaction weighting and user load for the tests accomplished. This indicates the approximate frequency at which the specific types of transactions where performed by the benchmark tool.

Due to network issues, configuration issues, and other items beyond control of the test team, over one hundred runs of the benchmark where done in order to complete the testing.

TRANSACTIONS

Transaction	Weight
Delivery Transaction	4
Payment Transaction	43
Stock-Level Transaction	4
Order-Status Transaction	4
New Order Transaction	45

USER LOADS

10
20
30
40
50
60
80
100
120
140
160
180
200
240
270
300
325
350
375
400
425
450
475
500
525
550
575
600

Table 4.3: *Transaction Weights and User Load Profile*

Testing

The initial testing was performed using two desktop and two laptop computers configured with the Benchmark Factory agents centrally coordinated by one of the laptops which was also running the Benchmark Factory main program. These desktop test systems where located in Alpharetta, Georgia remotely from the main Oracle10g RAC cluster located in Houston, Texas and all communication was via the web. The specifications for the test bed machines are shown in Table 4.4.

VIRTUAL STATION ID	STATION ID	NAME	MEMORY	PROCESSPR	# OF CPUs	OS	OS VERSION	OS BUILD
1	3	Test3	654828	Pentium(R)	2	Microsoft Windows 2000	Version: 5.0	2195
2	4	Test4	523760	Pentium(R)	1	Microsoft Windows 2000	Version: 5.0	2195
3	1	Test1	1046000	Pentium(R)	1	Microsoft Windows XP	Version: 5.1	2600
4	2	Test2	556528	Pentium(R)	1	Microsoft Windows 2000	Version: 5.0	2195

Table 4.4: *Test bed Configuration*

For mobile testing, the Test1 server was utilized.

Load balancing across the cluster was performed by the Oracle10g built-in load balancing algorithms and connections were made through a standard *tnsnames* connection via OracleNet. This configuration is shown below.

```
SSD1 =
  (DESCRIPTION =
    (ADDRESS = (PROTOCOL = TCP)(HOST = localhost)(PORT = 15212))
    (CONNECT_DATA =
      (SERVER = DEDICATED)
      (SERVICE_NAME = ssd)
      (INSTANCE_NAME = ssd1)
    )
  )

SSD2 =
  (DESCRIPTION =
    (ADDRESS = (PROTOCOL = TCP)(HOST = localhost)(PORT = 15213))
    (CONNECT_DATA =
      (SERVER = DEDICATED)
      (SERVICE_NAME = ssd)
      (INSTANCE_NAME = ssd2)
    )
  )

LISTENERS_SSD =
  (ADDRESS_LIST =
    (ADDRESS = (PROTOCOL = TCP)(HOST = localhost)(PORT = 15212))
    (ADDRESS = (PROTOCOL = TCP)(HOST = localhost)(PORT = 15213))
  )

SSD =
  (DESCRIPTION =
    (ADDRESS = (PROTOCOL = TCP)(HOST = localhost)(PORT = 15212))
    (ADDRESS = (PROTOCOL = TCP)(HOST = localhost)(PORT = 15213))
    (LOAD_BALANCE = yes)
    (CONNECT_DATA =
      (SERVER = DEDICATED)
      (SERVICE_NAME = ssd)
      (FAILOVER_MODE =
        (TYPE = SELECT)
        (METHOD = BASIC)
        (RETRIES = 180)
        (DELAY = 5)
      )
    )
  )
```

Notice that the host is set at localhost and the ports are not the standard 1521 ports, this is because port forwarding was utilized to allow tunneling through the TMS firewall.

The kernel was reconfigured with the suggested Oracle memory and network configuration via a startup file, which is shown below.

```
#!/bin/bash
#kconfig shell script
#chkconfig: 345 80 80
#description: Oracle Kernel configuration script
# /etc/init.d/kconfig
# Description: Performs kernel config for Oracle
# See how we were called.
```

```
case "$1" in
  start)
echo "300 32000 100 128">/proc/sys/kernel/sem
echo "2147483648">/proc/sys/kernel/shmmax
echo "2097152">/proc/sys/kernel/shmall
echo "4096">/proc/sys/kernel/shmmni
echo '262144'>/proc/sys/net/core/rmem_default
echo '262144'>/proc/sys/net/core/rmem_max
echo '262144'>/proc/sys/net/core/wmem_default
echo '262144'>/proc/sys/net/core/wmem_max
echo '4096 65536 4194304'>/proc/sys/net/ipv4/tcp_wmem
echo '4096 87380 4194304'>/proc/sys/net/ipv4/tcp_rmem
echo "1024 65000">/proc/sys/net/ipv4/ip_local_port_range
load_ocfs
mount -t ocfs /dev/sda1 /oracle
mount -t ocfs /dev/sdb1 /oracle2
;;
 stop)
;;
*)
echo "Usage: kconfig {start|stop}"
     exit 1
esac
exit 0
```

Other than these settings, all other settings were left at their default values. The next listing shows the non-default initialization parameter settings used during the test for the Oracle10g instance.

```
init.ora Parameters  DB/Inst: SSD/ssd2  Snaps: 1-2
                                                    End value
Parameter Name              Begin value             (if different)
---------------------------  ------------------------------  --------------
__db_cache_size             805306368
__java_pool_size            4194304
__large_pool_size           4194304
__shared_pool_size          255852544
background_dump_dest        /home/oracle/app/oracle/admin/ssd
cluster_database            TRUE
cluster_database_instances  2
compatible                  10.1.0.2.0
control_files               /oracle2/oradata/ssd/control01.ct
core_dump_dest              /home/oracle/app/oracle/admin/ssd
db_block_size               8192
db_domain
db_file_multiblock_read_count 16
db_name                     ssd
dispatchers                 (PROTOCOL=TCP) (SERVICE=ssdXDB)
instance_number             2
job_queue_processes         10
open_cursors                300
pga_aggregate_target        356515840
processes                   800
remote_listener             LISTENERS_SSD
remote_login_passwordfile   EXCLUSIVE
sga_target                  1073741824
spfile                      /oracle2/oradata/ssd/spfilessd.or
thread                      2
undo_management             AUTO
undo_tablespace             UNDOTBS2
user_dump_dest              /home/oracle/app/oracle/admin/ssd
            ---------------------------------------------------------
```

The only parameters altered during testing where *sga_max_size* and *sga_target*. They were set at 1G, 500M, 250M for the three phases of the testing and Oracle was allowed to use the Automatic Memory Management (AMM) feature to internally alter memory structures as needed.

Many TPC-C tests utilize larger test databases, however, the memory of this test configuration was a total of 4 gigabytes and the test team intended to only utilize 2-3 gigabytes of this memory for the Oracle system to allow for large numbers of users. In addition the test team wanted to demonstrate what occurs with RAID as more and more of the data is moved from memory to disk on the RAID and with SSD in the same situation. This desire to test the affects of full and partial caching resulted in the need for a small footprint database, one which could be completely cached in the virtual memory space provided by the cluster and one that would respond to the reduction of that memory forcing more and more disk activity. Utilization of a TPC-C schema that was many times larger than the available memory would have resulted in not being able to test the affects of full caching and partial caching of the data.

In order to test the effects of full caching and partial caching the test team re-ran the TPC-C tests with configurations of 250 megabyte SGA, 500 megabyte SGA and 1 gigabyte SGA sizes using the automatic memory management settings for *sga_target* and *sga_max_size* of the Oracle 10g server on both the RAID and SSD arrays.

The TPC-C benchmark utilizes a basic 9 table schema consisting of a typical OLTP scenario utilizing warehouses, sales, and other point-of-sale type tables. The schema tables are shown in Appendix A. The Benchmark Factory software generates both the schema and the data load. Table 4.5 shows the number of rows in each of the schema tables.

TABLE	OCCURRENCES
C_CUSTOMER	480,000
C_DISTRICT	160
C_HISTORY	622,113
C_ITEM	100,000
C_NEW_ORDER	169,556
C_ORDER	633,769
C_ORDER_LINE	6,340,427
C_STOCK	1,600,000
C_WAREHOUSE	16

Table 4.5: *Table Row Counts*

Insert and Delete Operations

It must be ascertained that insert and/or delete operations to any of the tables can occur concurrently with the TPC-C transaction mix. Furthermore, any restrictions in the SUT database implementation that precludes inserts beyond the limits defined in Clause 1.4.11 must be disclosed. This includes the maximum number of rows that can be inserted and the minimum key value for these new rows.

All insert and delete functions were verified to be fully operational during the entire benchmark.

Partitioning

While there are a few restrictions placed on horizontal or vertical partitioning of tables and rows in the TPC-C benchmark, any such partitioning must be disclosed.

No partitioning was used.

Replication, Duplication or Additions

Replication of tables, if used, must be disclosed. Additional and/or duplicated attributes in any table must be disclosed along with a statement on the impact on performance.

No replications, duplications or additional attributes were used in this benchmark.

Random Number Generation

The method of verification for the random number generation must be described.

The Benchmark Factory tool internally generated random numbers as needed. The actual methodology used was not disclosed by Quest.

Results

Never accept bold claims without examining proof!

As with everything else, the proof is in the numbers. The following examines the actual results from multiple TPC-C runs on the test systems using both RAID and SSD infrastructures.

The results showed clearly that in a CPU driven system with the full database cached the performance of the system is dependent on the number, speed, and capacity of the CPUs and the latency and bandwidth of the interconnect. Look at the comparison between the two setups (RAID and SSD) in a fully cached state in Figure 4.3.

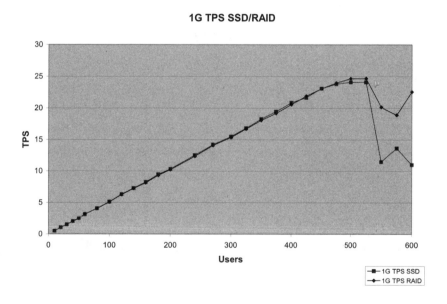

Figure 4.3: *Comparison of RAID to SSD with Full Caching*

This figure illustrates how the transactions per second (TPS) are virtually identical with the same maximum TPS inflection point for both the RAID and SSD system configurations. This demonstrates that as the database becomes fully-cached the response of the system is less dependent on the I/O subsystem and more dependent upon the memory and CPU and in the case of real application clusters, the speed of the interconnect.

Next will be an examination of the results for each interface: RAID and SSD.

RAID Results

RAID results are referring to standard disk based systems whether they are standard RAID, SATA or other interfaces that map into the RAID framework. The major result from a TPC-C result is throughput, measured as transactions per second. RAID test throughput will be examined first.

RAID Throughput

As memory was decreased from 1 gigabyte first to 500 megabytes and then to 250 megabytes, the RAID system responded as expected with less overall throughput as more and more disk I/O was performed. This is shown in Figure 4.4.

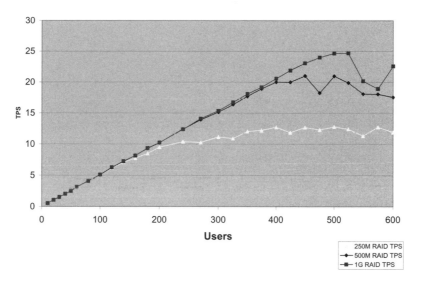

Figure 4.4: *RAID TPS graph for Various Memory Configurations*

This shows that as the disk plays a more active roll in the transaction base, the latency involved in disk operations causes a net reduction in throughput. Another measure is bytes per second, and that will be presented next.

RAID Bytes per Second

When bytes per second (BPS) for RAID are examined, the same decreasing profile can be seen. This decrease in BPS as memory is reduced is of course expected as the number of transactions decreases. This is shown in Figure 4.5.

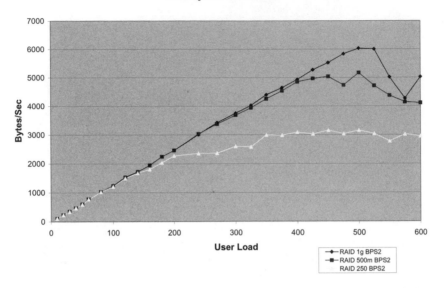

Figure 4.5: *RAID Bytes per Second for Various Memory Configurations*

This shows that as the RAID environment becomes more and more dependent on the disk I/O subsystem, the transaction rate and rate of data flow decrease dramatically on a per user basis. Essentially, for a given user load that exceeds the breakpoint this breaks down to a simple equation:

```
TPSf = TPSi * (RBPT/IOR)*Q
```

Where:

- TPSf – Transactions per second final

- TPSi – Transactions per second Initial (Peak with 100% caching)

- RBPT – Required bytes per transaction per second

- IOR – Sustained Bytes IO rate in bytes per second

- Q – A constant that takes into account other latency factors which should be a constant for a given configuration.

The breakpoint is the point of inflection for a given TPS curve.

So for a RAID based system the transactions will never be more than what can be achieved in a fully cached situation assuming that the interconnect latency is much less than the overall disk latency.

RAID Average Transaction Time

The performance behavior is inverted when average transaction time is considered. As memory in a RAID based system is decreased, average transaction time increases. As more processes contend for limited disk I/O capability, the average transaction time must increase resulting in fewer transactions per second and lower bytes per second. This is shown in Figure 4.6.

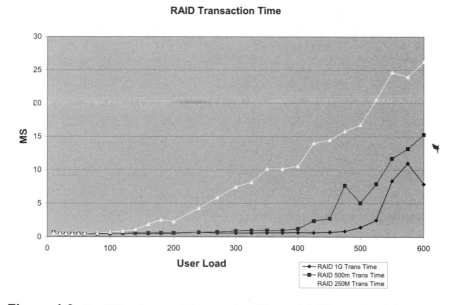

Figure 4.6: *RAID Average Transaction Time with Decreasing Memory*

RAID Average Response Time

The final results for the RAID tests show the average response time. As would be expected, as the memory decreases, forcing more dependence on disk, the response time increases, just as with average transaction times. This is shown in Figure 4.7.

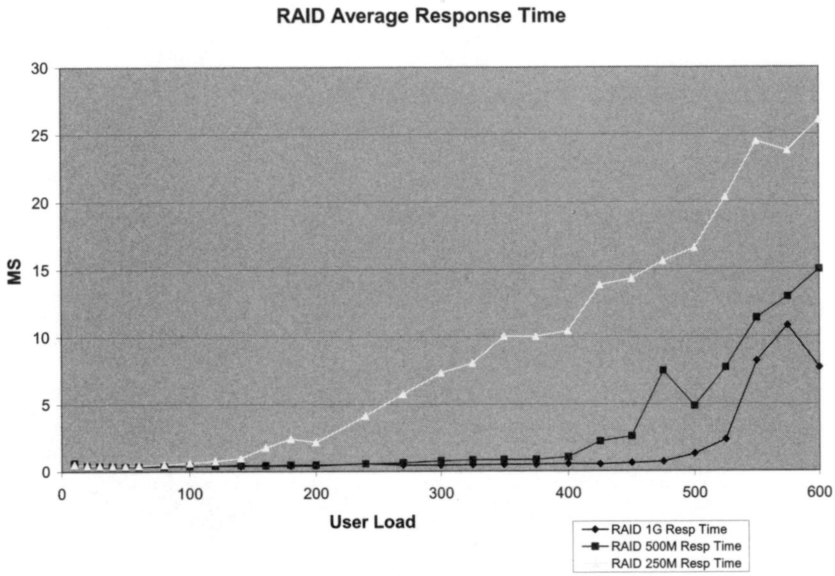

RAID Average Response Time

Figure 4.7: *RAID Average Response Time with Decreasing Memory*

As expected, all performance indicators showed poorer performance in a disk-based system as available cache memory decreased. This decrease in performance is caused directly by increasing disk contention thereby forcing high latency times and queuing to occur on the underlying disks.

The same tests were performed using solid-state disk technology and those results will be examined next.

SSD Results

The SSD results using the RamSan400 were anything but typical. Remember that the RAC systems tested were identical down to the host bus adapter (HBA). The only variable was whether the RAID or SSD system was used.

SSD Throughput

As with the RAID system, the transactions per second (TPS) will be examined as the amount of server memory is decreased. This drives I/O to the RamSan-400. Figure 4.8 shows the results from this decrease in server cache memory.

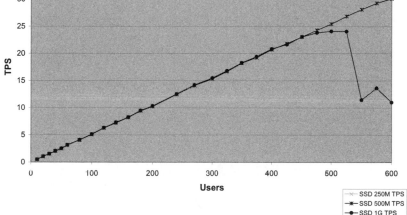

Figure 4.8: *SSD TPS with Decreasing Memory*

As I/O is forced to the RamSan-400, the TPS actually increases. This is because the I/O speed of the RamSan-400 is actually

---

much better than the latency of the RAC high-speed interconnect. The interconnect speed is the primary driving factor in the fully cached system as the transactions are limited by the amount of data that must be transferred and the latency of the interconnect. With the non-fully cached server the number of transactions is dependent more upon the speed of the underlying I/O subsystem. Hence, when a system exists with I/O speed that is faster than the interconnect latency, the TPS is increased by driving I/O away from the interconnect and to the I/O subsystem!

SSD Bytes per Second

What about bytes per second? Figure 4.9 shows the results from decreasing the per-instance server memory for a RamSan-400 based system. As the memory in the server that was allocated to Oracle was decreased by resetting the *sga_max_size* and *sga_target* settings in the SSD based test, bytes per second increased. Figure 4.9 shows the results on total bytes per second from decreasing the per-instance memory for a RamSan-400 based system.

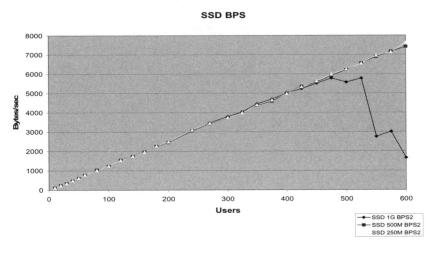

Figure 4.9: *SSD Bytes per Second with Decreasing Memory*

This figure shows how the bytes-per-second increases as dependency on the interconnect is removed and the system moves away from being fully cached when using SSD technology. This is due to the factor of ten or more difference between the average latencies of the cluster interconnect and the speed of reads and writes on the SSD system.

SSD Average Transaction Time

Perhaps the most dramatic difference is in the average transaction time results when comparing the RAID to the SSD system. As expected from a review of the previous SSD results, a decrease in the average transaction time should be expected allowing more transactions and more bytes per second. However, a very dramatic decrease as cache memory was reduced was seen. Look at Figure 4.10.

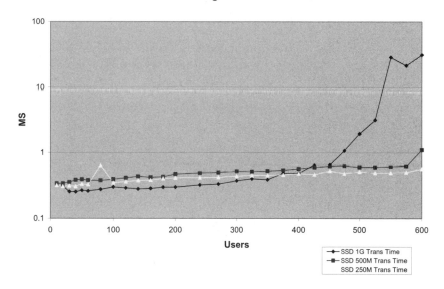

Figure 4.10: *SSD Average Transaction Time With Decreasing Memory*

Once dependence on the interconnect is mitigated, the transaction times dramatically improved by several orders of magnitude. The scale on the graph in Figure 4.10 is logarithmic. This means that for one increase in scale on the vertical axis, an increase by a factor of 10 can be seen. Compare the average transaction times in Figure 4.10 to those from the RAID tests in Figure 4.6. The dramatic difference between the two technologies can be seen as memory is reduced. This indicates that by utilizing the RamSan400 SSD system transaction times were improved by nearly a factor of 100, two orders of magnitude!

SSD Average Response Times

Since the average response time is dependent on transaction times, the results for the RamSan400 mirror those for average transaction time is shown in Figure 4.11.

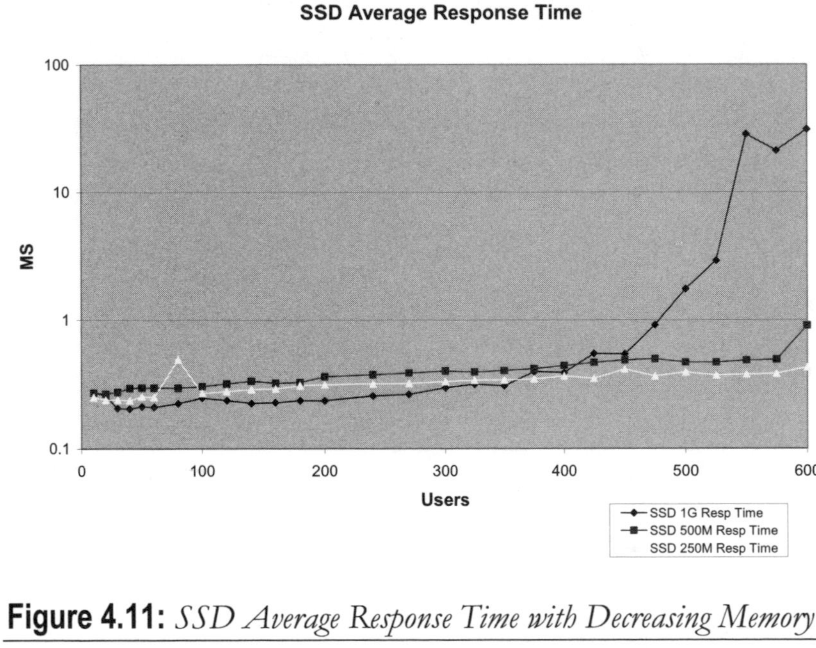

Figure 4.11: *SSD Average Response Time with Decreasing Memory*

Again note the logarithmic vertical scale. As with average transaction time, a nearly 2 order of magnitude difference can be seen when the latency of the RAC high-speed interconnect is mitigated as a factor in response time. Comparing the RAID average response time in Figure 4.7 to SSD average response time in Figure 4.11 also highlights the dramatic difference between the two storage subsystems.

Conclusion

In Summary SSD in low, medium or high doses is good for RAC!

In an Oracle10g RAC based system, as the amount of data cached reaches the maximum, the performance becomes dependent on the latency and bandwidth of the interconnect and the speed of the CPUs and memory of the systems involved in the RAC cluster. As the amount of memory decreases and thus the amount of cached data decreases, the performance is directly dependent on the latency and bandwidth of the I/O subsystem.

In the case of a typical RAID disk based system with minimal caching, a net decrease in performance can be expected as the amount of cached data decreases. This decrease in performance is reflected in the overall throughput or transactions per second, bytes transferred, and response and transaction times.

In the case where the RAID subsystem is replaced by a solid state disk system such as the RamSan-400, the system throughput, bytes transferred, transaction and response times improve, sometimes dramatically, depending upon how much less the latency and greater the bandwidth of the RamSan-400 is compared to the latency of the RAC interconnect.

Therefore, in an Oracle10g RAC system that is based on a typical RAID disk system the goal should be to cache as much data as possible in the database cache to improve performance and response. However, in a RamSan or solid state disk system (memory disks) improvement will be seen in performance and response times by actually reducing the amount of server cache and driving I/O to the solid state disk array as long as the high-speed interconnect latency is greater than that of the solid state disk subsystem.

Therefore, in an Oracle0g RAC system that is based on a typical RAID system, the goal should be to cache as much data as possible in the database cache to improve performance and response.

To provide further points of comparison in the study of the use of SATA or SCSI arrays and the use of solid state technology with Oracle, the next chapter will take a look at a TPC-H benchmark with Oracle9i and SSD.

TPC-H Warehouse Benchmark With SSD

In Chapter 4, the results from a TPC-C test with Oracle10g and RAC were shown. This chapter is designed to give a perspective on how solid-state disk (SSD) may affect the decision support or data warehouse type database on Oracle. The results from testing using Oracle9i utilizing a TPC-H benchmark will be shown. The TPC-H benchmark uses tools provided by TPC organization to generate data loads and standard queries. These tools are the *dbgen* and *qgen* utilities.

Query Processing

The *qgen* program produces 22 example decision support system (DSS) queries. The queries use aggregation, subqueries, order bys and group bys to simulate the processing in a DSS environment. The queries were placed into a single file and run back-to-back in the tests. STATSPACK and custom scripts were used to monitor the database.

SSD Results

In the SSD test runs, the following configurations were tested:

- Base run to load buffers
- No logging on all tables and no archive log setting
- No logging on all tables with archive logging
- Logging and archive logging

The SSD runs showed very constant times for all the various configurations after query eight was run in the base load run number one. This type of profile recurred after a shutdown startup, as shown in the graph in Figure 5.1. The entire set of seven total runs only required three days to process from May 28, 2004 through June 1, 2004. These were not run back-to-back but as time allowed. Figure 5.1 shows the comparisons of the various SSD configurations.

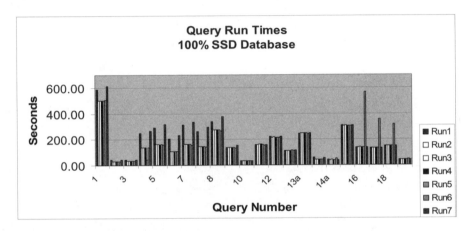

Figure 5.1: *SSD Query Run Times*

As shown in Figure 5.1, even the poorest performing query, query number one, required just more than 600 seconds to complete in its worst run, run number seven. The complete query timings are shown in Table 5.1. Run number six, with archive logging turned on, showed nearly identical query timing results as compared with previous runs, until the next to last three queries. After a restart, query number seven showed similar performance to run number one, even with archive logging turned on. The three poorly, relative to the other SSD runs, performing queries returned to normal performance levels.

Using the SSD array, the use of logging and archive logging had little or no effect on performance.

SCSI Runs

The SCSI runs required from June 2, 2004 to July 30, 2004 to complete. This 58 day period encompassed seven full query runs and a single partial run. This was with queries running as close as possible to 24X7, between equipment failures and connectivity issues. During the test, the initial 2-disk SCSI array failed during the second query set run. This required a database rebuild and reload on the provided ATA array. After the SCSI failure, the entire initial query run had to be repeated, compared to the SCSI results and the decision was made at that time to discard the SCSI results and continue with the ATA array.

The initial *nologging* and *noarchiving* runs performed so poorly that *nologging* and *noarchivelogging* set points were used during the subsequent tests as well to allow the tests to complete in a reasonable amount of time. This is due to the fact that turning on *logging* and *archivelog* would further stress the I/O subsystem resulting in even poorer performance. The following issues further complicated the testing:

- When running the queries against the 100% SCSI/ATA database, query number one would not complete, and after 30 hours it was halted.

- When running the queries against the 100% SCSI/ATA database, query number four would not complete in 30 hours, and it was halted.

- When running against the 100% SCSI/ATA database query number produced the error codes shown below. It then terminated the session causing all subsequent queries to fail in run number one, requiring a restart:

```
Sun Jun  6 11:43:16 2004
Errors in file /home/oracle/admin/dss/udump/dss_ora_615.trc:
ORA-00600: internal error code, arguments: [kftts2bz_many_files], [0], [39218], [],
[], [], [], []
Sun Jun  6 11:43:17 2004
Errors in file /home/oracle/admin/dss/udump/dss_ora_615.trc:
ORA-07445: exception encountered: core dump [kghbigasp()+289] [SIGSEGV] [Address not
mapped to object] [0x427A8] [] []
ORA-00600: internal error code, arguments: [kftts2bz_many_files], [0], [39218], [],
[], [], [], []
Sun Jun  6 11:43:18 2004
Errors in file /home/oracle/admin/dss/udump/dss_ora_615.trc:
ORA-07445: exception encountered: core dump [kghbigasp()+289] [SIGSEGV] [Address not
mapped to object] [0x427A8] [] []
ORA-07445: exception encountered: core dump [kghbigasp()+289] [SIGSEGV] [Address not
mapped to object] [0x427A8] [] []
ORA-00600: internal error code, arguments: [kftts2bz_many_files], [0], [39218], [],
[], [], [], []
Sun Jun  6 11:43:18 2004
Errors in file /home/oracle/admin/dss/udump/dss_ora_615.trc:
ORA-07445: exception encountered: core dump [kghbigasp()+289] [SIGSEGV] [Address not
mapped to object] [0x427A8] [] []
ORA-07445: exception encountered: core dump [kghbigasp()+289] [SIGSEGV] [Address not
mapped to object] [0x427A8] [] []
ORA-07445: exception encountered: core dump [kghbigasp()+289] [SIGSEGV] [Address not
mapped to object] [0x427A8] [] []
ORA-00600: internal error code, arguments: [kftts2bz_many_files], [0], [39218], [],
[], [], [], []
[oracle@AMD43 bdump]$
[oracle@AMD43 bdump]$ tail -f alert_dss.log
Errors in file /home/oracle/admin/dss/udump/dss_ora_615.trc:
ORA-07445: exception encountered: core dump [kghbigasp()+289] [SIGSEGV] [Address not
mapped to object] [0x427A8] [] []
ORA-07445: exception encountered: core dump [kghbigasp()+289] [SIGSEGV] [Address not
mapped to object] [0x427A8] [] []
ORA-00600: internal error code, arguments: [kftts2bz_many_files], [0], [39218], [],
[], [], [], []
Sun Jun  6 11:43:18 2004
Errors in file /home/oracle/admin/dss/udump/dss_ora_615.trc:
ORA-07445: exception encountered: core dump [kghbigasp()+289] [SIGSEGV] [Address not
mapped to object] [0x427A8] [] []
ORA-07445: exception encountered: core dump [kghbigasp()+289] [SIGSEGV] [Address not
mapped to object] [0x427A8] [] []
ORA-07445: exception encountered: core dump [kghbigasp()+289] [SIGSEGV] [Address not
mapped to object] [0x427A8] [] []
ORA-00600: internal error code, arguments: [kftts2bz_many_files], [0], [39218], [],
[], [], [], []
```

- The queries would run out of temporary space, undo segment space, and generate the above errors if run back-to-back in the same user. The script running the queries was modified to include a new connect statement before each query, releasing previous *undo* segments and *temp* segments for reuse. This was not required in the SSD tests. Each run was actually several smaller runs restarted at the point of failure.

- During run number two of the initial SCSI test, the array failed after approximately eight days of 24X7 processing. This required the rebuild of the database on the new ATA array.

- During the final runs, a complete power outage that caused a reassignment of the ATA array address, which resulted in two days of down time. The data was fully recovered through the automated recovery processing and the testing resumed.

- Several days were also lost due to connectivity issues.

- Any query that required longer than ~30 hours was terminated and processing restarted at the next query in the file. This was required on queries number one, three, 13, 13a, 17, and 18 in various configurations. The resulting time was set to 1440 minutes (24 hours) and the graph axis set to logarithmic to allow the graphs to show at least some of the shorter query times.

ATA Configurations

The ATA array was tested for the following configurations:

- *nologging* and *noarchive* base run

- *nologging* and *noarchive*

- Logs and temp files on SSD

- Data on SSD full buffer memory (1 gigabyte)

- Data on SSD half buffer memory (500 megabytes)

The results for the queries are shown in Figure 5.2. The percentage difference between SSD and SATA are so large it does not make sense to even report them; however, the total elapsed times, adding in a base of 1,440 minutes per each non-complete query for the SCSI, show a factor of 179 times difference between the SSD and ATA results in favor of the SSD drives. The queries for the SSD tests all completed, while several in the ATA tests were halted at the 24 hour point.

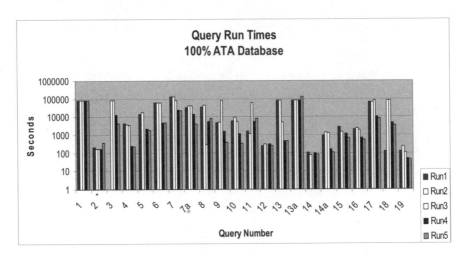

Figure 5.2: *ATA Run Times*

In order to plot the results on a single plot, the vertical scale had to be switched to logarithmic; therefore, the changes in query time may only appear to be slight on the graph but may actually be several tens of percentage points. The runs not involving the SSD showed consistent results.

When the *temp* and *undo* tablespaces were moved to the SSD drives some queries improved, while others got worse. When the *data* tablespace was moved to SSD all query times were improved by an average of 100 percent. The reduction of *db_cache_size* by half with the *data* tablespace on SSD actually show some improvements in performance on queries number two, eight, 11, 13, and 13a, while the others performed worse than the full memory levels. However, all of the queries performed better with the data on the SSD than the ones on 100% ATA.

Comparing the Different Scenarios

During this series of runs, many things where tested. Of course at the most basic level, the raw performance of SSD versus disk technology was the main item tested, but other scenarios were also tested:

- SSD performance with the DSS type queries with *nologging* and *noarchivelogging*

- SSD Performance with the DSS type queries with *logging* and *archivelogging*

- Regular Disk Performance for DSS type queries with *nologging* and *noarchivelogging*

- Regular Disk performance for DSS type queries with *NL* and *NAL* and temporary and undo segments on SSD

- Regular disk performance for DSS type queries with *NL* and *NAL* and data on the SSD

- Regular disk performance for DSS type queries with NL and NAL and memory reduced.

SSD Scenario Comparisons

Overall SSD performance was uniform, except for the initial run when memory areas used in later queries were being loaded. Assuming that the data loaded and then read from Oracle memory structures was nearly identical for each set of identical queries with identical initialization parameters, the SSD out performed the regular disks for DSS queries by at least two orders of magnitude.

In comparing the total time for all queries to complete, the SSD database out performed the normal disk databases by a minimum factor of 179. Several of the normal disk queries had to be halted at the 24 hour point in order to be able to complete the query runs in a reasonable time period. Therefore, the true magnitude of the differences in times between the SSD and normal disk runs

---

is in reality much higher. Table 5.1 lists the results from the seven SSD runs:

SSD query	Run1	Run2	Run3	Run4	Run5	Run6	Run7
1	589.94	501.53	502.47	500.54	501.06	507.31	615.21
2	42.24	30.83	30.76	30.44	30.37	30.55	43.18
3	41.55	34.72	35.54	34.83	35.49	35.35	40.86
4	249.30	139.02	139.30	139.42	42.04	136.11	267.70
5	292.28	161.48	162.43	160.54	161.17	158.40	317.08
6	205.12	107.87	109.20	108.88	108.78	107.37	230.25
7	314.09	161.59	162.83	162.01	162.14	156.74	334.97
7a	263.43	144.45	145.12	145.42	144.85	139.88	297.13
8	340.17	272.98	274.20	273.95	273.32	267.27	379.45
9	137.69	137.40	138.78	137.62	138.40	134.25	154.53
10	35.20	35.46	35.72	35.51	35.49	35.28	36.19
11	157.74	159.13	161.64	161.27	160.43	154.48	160.75
12	224.77	215.71	217.33	214.72	215.66	214.58	225.20
13	113.01	113.16	113.79	113.76	113.93	111.85	114.70
13a	246.45	248.79	250.66	249.36	250.39	238.84	249.17
14	57.98	44.32	42.82	41.95	42.04	42.19	54.56
14a	42.49	40.66	40.91	40.50	40.34	50.65	39.86
15	309.07	306.37	308.89	306.73	306.27	305.89	307.92
16	138.37	138.70	140.02	138.65	139.12	565.86	138.11
17	133.08	133.53	134.41	133.71	133.36	355.08	132.71
18	149.93	150.41	150.93	150.86	150.56	319.14	149.90
19	43.58	44.03	44.44	43.41	43.19	47.45	43.35
Total	4127.48	3322.14	3342.19	3324.08	3228.40	4114.52	4332.78

Table 5.1: *SSD Query Timings for all Runs*

SCSI/ATA Scenario Comparisons

In the SCSI/ATA query runs, there was more diversity in the results as shown in Table 5.2.

SCSI query	Run1	Run2	Run3	Run4	Run5
1	86400.00	86400.00	86400.00	86400.00	86400.00
2	207.62	161.84	162.90	165.08	358.03
3	0.00	86400.00	86400.00	12657.46	4317.06
4	4313.82	3666.76	3372.94	243.31	228.24
5	13568.08	17804.46	0.00	2145.11	1912.33
6	61926.08	61367.15	61547.58	4823.09	4581.85
7	133456.46	132743.60	86400.00	23259.28	22497.74
7a	33038.67	40758.41	41817.98	13807.28	4158.16
8	36062.61	46331.87	284.91	5361.54	8134.71
9	4779.68	5138.53	86400.00	1550.05	406.09
10	6125.83	9278.53	5544.37	1164.96	347.61
11	1650.96	1144.37	62632.58	5602.72	8191.45
12	249.64	319.86	0.00	300.85	256.31
13	86400.00	86400.00	5283.60	444.54	457.22
13a	86400.00	86400.00	86400.00	86400.00	131326.99
14	106.79	75.49	0.00	94.00	86.51
14a	917.28	1323.80	1228.10	154.44	108.91
15	2803.80	1511.22	0.00	1205.10	690.55
16	1958.00	2309.16	1909.33	662.30	519.49
17	65826.95	66631.73	86400.00	10388.28	7947.97
18	118.65	86400.00	86400.00	4597.52	3471.07
19	120.06	222.30	100.90	49.91	46.28
Total Sec	626430.98	822789.08	788693.27	261476.82	286444.57
Total Days	7.25	9.52	9.13	3.03	3.32

Table 5.2: *Comparisons of the SCSI/ATA Runs*

Standard SCSI/ATA Runs

Runs number one and two were standard query runs with the exception they were done as *nologging* and *noarchivelog* mode. In many cases, run times for query number one, with a couple of notable differences, were longer than run number two due to increased need for disk reads to populate the data cache in the Oracle memory system.

Run Three with Temporary and Undo on SSD

Run three placed the *temporary* and *undo* segments on the SSD array. This improved the response time for queries that used a lot of sorts or hash joins such as eight, ten and 13, allowing 13 to finish in less than 24 hours, but overall the gains did not outweigh the losses.

Run Four with DATA on SSD

In run four, the data segments were moved to the SSD, and the temporary and undo segments were placed back on normal drives. The total run time improved by a factor of three, three days versus nine days, even allowing for the two queries that still could not complete. In many cases, the run times improved by an order of magnitude.

Run Five with Data on SSD and Reduced Memory

In an effort to gauge the importance of setting *db cache size* when using SSD assets, in run five the *db_cache_size* was reduced by 50% from one gigabyte to 500 megabytes. The results were surprising in that the overall run time, if query 13a is set to the 86,400 value instead of its actual time, was reduced by eight percent with most queries showing some improvement in runtime. However, this may be an artifact of several queries that did not complete before having completed during run four and populated the smaller cache with useful data. This would be one area of additional research for future work.

Conclusion

In the SSD verses ATA benchmark, the gains for INSERT and UPDATE processing as shown in the database loading and index build scenarios was a respectable 30%. This 30% was due to the CPU overhead involved in the INSERT and UPDATE activities. If the Oracle level processing for INSERT and UPDATE activities could be optimized for SSD, significant performance gains might be realized during these activities.

The most significant performance gain comes in the use of SSD in query-based transaction loads. The performance gains for using SSD can be quite spectacular. Improvement factors of 176 times better performance over standard disk technologies are documented in the report.

Even when only data files can be placed on SSD assets, the performance gains are phenomenal, up to or greater than 300%, as also shown in the benchmarks.

Now that various benchmarks with Oracle, SSD, and disk technologies have been explored, the following chapter looks at how SSD technology can be utilized in specific systems. The next chapter will examine how to determine if the system would benefit from SSD technology and the various configuration options available.

Oracle Tuning With Selective Application of SSD

Analyzing What to Put On SSD

Now that it has been demonstrated that SSD technology can be a great help to most types of systems, how can users determine if their system is one of them? This chapter will provide insight into the methods used to analyze a system to determine if SSD technology will help it.

The choices of what to put on the SSD drive break down into several general areas:

- Data

- Indexes

- Redo logs

- Temporary files

Generally speaking, files such as control files and archive logs are not a performance issue, so their placement is not as critical as the above listed files.

So how does one determine what files should be placed on SSD arrays? The following section will introduce some analysis tools.

Analysis Tools

Analysis to determine what to place on SSD files falls under two categories, operating system level analysis and Oracle internal analysis. Both methods involve analyzing the I/O wait interface from either the system or Oracle perspective.

In many situations, the operating system level analysis may be inconclusive due to the combining of physical disks into large, RAID combined logical disks. In this case, the I/O to the individual datafiles from the Oracle perspective must get a good look.

Inside Oracle, there are two areas to look at to determine the best candidates for placement on the SSD asset. These two are the I/O statistics and the wait interface statistics. Looking at the I/O interface for average I/O times and total I/O to specific datafiles helps determine usage patterns for datafiles and temp files. Looking at the wait interface helps determine if processes are waiting on I/O related events and what events are being waited on.

The analyst has several possible sources for the I/O and wait interface statistics:

- Custom scripts
- Oracle Enterprise Manager
- Third-party tools
- AWRPRT reports

The use of custom scripts gives the analyst control over the selection and display of specific statistics of concern. Oracle Enterprise Manager (OEM) provides a plethora of data but may not be available at all sites. Third-party tools also provide a wealth of data but are expensive and may not be installed at all client locations. STATSPACK reports are available at all sites, provide a wealth of statistics and allow a focused look at specific time intervals.

Of the available data gathering methods, scripts and STATSPACK will be the focus in this chapter.

Custom Scripts

Generally speaking, custom scripts utilize the *v$* series of views to generate reports showing I/O distribution, timing data and wait statistics. For data and temp file related statistics, the *v$filestat* and *v$tempstat* tables are utilized. For wait interface information, the *v$waitstat*, *v$sysstat* and *v$sesstat* tables can be utilized. The following is an example script for generating I/O related data:

🖫 **IO_data.sql**

```
-- ***************************************************
-- Copyright © 2005 by Rampant TechPress
-- This script is free for non-commercial purposes
-- with no warranties.  Use at your own risk.
--
-- To license this script for a commercial purpose,
-- contact info@rampant.cc
-- ***************************************************
column inst_id format 999 heading 'Ins'
column sum_io1 new_value st1 noprint
column sum_io2 new_value st2 noprint
column sum_io new_value divide_by noprint
column Percent format 99.9 heading 'Perc|Of I/O'
column brratio format 999.99 heading 'Blck|Read|Rat'
column bwratio format 999.99 heading 'Blck|Write|Rat'
column phyrds heading 'Phys|Reads'
column phywrts heading 'Phys|Writes'
column phyblkrd heading 'Phys|Block|Reads'
column phyblkwrt heading 'Phys|Block|Writes'
column name format a45 heading 'File|Name'
column file# format 9999 heading 'File'
set feedback off verify off lines 132 pages 60 sqlbl on trims on
rem
select
     nvl(sum(a.phyrds+a.phywrts),0) sum_io1
from
     sys.gv_$filestat a;
select nvl(sum(b.phyrds+b.phywrts),0) sum_io2
from
        sys.gv_$tempstat b;
select &st1+&st2 sum_io from dual;
rem
ttitle 'File I/O Statistics Report'
spool fileio
select
     a.inst_id, a.file#,b.name, a.phyrds, a.phywrts,
     (100*(a.phyrds+a.phywrts)/&divide_by) Percent,
```

```
    a.phyblkrd, a.phyblkwrt, (a.phyblkrd/greatest(a.phyrds,1))
brratio,
     (a.phyblkwrt/greatest(a.phywrts,1)) bwratio
from
    sys.gv_$filestat a, sys.gv_$dbfile b
where
    a.file#=b.file#
and a.inst_id=b.inst_id
union
select
    c.inst_id, c.file#,d.name, c.phyrds, c.phywrts,
    (100*(c.phyrds+c.phywrts)/&divide_by) Percent,
    c.phyblkrd, c.phyblkwrt,(c.phyblkrd/greatest(c.phyrds,1))
brratio,
     (c.phyblkwrt/greatest(c.phywrts,1)) bwratio
from
    sys.gv_$tempstat c, sys.gv_$tempfile d
where
    c.file#=d.file#
 and c.inst_id=d.inst_id
order by 1,2;
spool off
pause Press enter to continue
set feedback on verify on lines 80 pages 22
clear columns
ttitle off
```

In this script, both the *gv$filestat* and *gv$tempstat* tables are utilized, and the results are compared to a total I/O figure so each datafile and tempfile's I/O is captured. In RAC, the *gv$* views contain statistics cumulative since the database started.

For Oracle RAC environments, the *gv$* version of these tables needs to be utilized so that total I/O across all instances is captured. The *v$* only captures statistics for the single instance. The following is an example of the output from the script for the TPCH environment with ATA drives:

```
Mon Jul 19                                                                    page    1
                          File I/O Statistics Report
                                                      Phys   Phys Blck Blck
         File                              Phys  Phys Perc  Block Block Read  Wrt
Ins File Name                              Reads Writes I/O  Reads Writes Rat  Rat
--- ---- ---------------------------------- -------- ------ ---- -------- ------ ----- -----
  1    1 /u08/oracle/oradata/dss/system01.dbf    12857   1201  .0    47975    1201 3.73  1.00
  1    1 /u12/oracle/oradata/dss/tem101.dbf       8733  25480  .0    80127  338717 9.18 13.29
  1    2 /u09/oracle/oradata/dss/undotbs101.dbf     50   2979  .0       50    2979 1.00  1.00
  1    2 /u12/oracle/oradata/dss/tem102.dbf          4      0  .0        4       0 1.00   .00
  1    3 /u12/oracle/oradata/dss/temp05.dbf          4      0  .0        4       0 1.00   .00
  1    3 /u12/oracle/oradata/dss/undotbs103.dbf     50    397  .0       50     397 1.00  1.00
  1    4 /u01/oracle/oradata/dss/temp021.dbf         0      0  .0        0       0 1.00   .00
  1    4 /u11/oracle/oradata/dss/undotbs102.dbf    313   3157  .0      313    3157 1.00  1.00
  1    5 /u02/oracle/oradata/dss/temp022.dbf         0      0  .0        0       0  .00   .00
  1    5 /u08/oracle/oradata/dss/dss_data01.dbf 33688717      3 35.6 34889652       3 1.04  1.00
  1    6 /u09/oracle/oradata/dss/dss_data02.dbf 29910924      3 31.6 31075321       3 1.04  1.00
  1    7 /u10/oracle/oradata/dss/dss_data03.dbf 30345274      3 32.0 31504507       3 1.04  1.00
  1    8 /u11/oracle/oradata/dss/dss_index01.dbf  182678      3  .1   243693       3 1.33  1.00
  1    9 /u13/oracle/oradata/dss/dss_index02.dbf  181979      3  .1   245391       3 1.35  1.00
  1   10 /u14/oracle/oradata/dss/dss_index03.dbf  173160      3  .1   233697       3 1.35  1.00
  1   11 /u09/oracle/oradata/dss/drsys01.dbf         5      3  .0        5       3 1.00  1.00
  1   12 /u09/oracle/oradata/dss/tools01.dbf         5      3  .0        5       3 1.00  1.00
  1   13 /u10/oracle/oradata/dss/xdb01.dbf          11      3  .0       23       3 2.09  1.00
```

```
1   14 /u13/oracle/oradata/dss/dss_index3.dbf      11554    3   .0    11554    3 1.00  1.00
1   15 /u10/oracle/oradata/dss_index05.dbf             5    3   .0        5    3 1.00  1.00
1   16 /u09/oracle/oradata/dss_index06.dbf             5    3   .0        5    3 1.00  1.00
1   17 /u08/oracle/oradata/dss_index07.dbf             5    3   .0        5    3 1.00  1.00
1   18 /u03/oracle/oradata/dss/undo021.dbf             0    3   .0        0    3  .00  1.00
1   19 /u04/oracle/oradata/dss/uno022.dbf              0    3   .0        0    3  .00  1.00
```

In this listing, the majority, a total of 98%, of I/O is being directed to the *dss_data* tablespace datafiles with the second largest contribution being the *dss_index* datafiles with 0.580 percent, and the temporary tablespace at 0.036 percent. From this report, one can see that the major stress is being placed on the *data* datafiles.

A look at the operating system *iostat* command confirms that the I/O subsystem is undergoing an extreme amount of stress. The listing below shows the results of an *iostat* command revealing the first set of data, which consists of the averages since system startup, have been omitted:

```
avg-cpu:  %user    %nice    %sys    %idle
           0.20     0.00     0.60   99.20

Device:            tps    Blk_read/s   Blk_wrtn/s   Blk_read   Blk_wrtn
dev3-0           59.04       854.62       269.88       2128        672
dev8-0            0.00         0.00         0.00          0          0
dev8-1         1795.18     14361.45         0.00      35760          0

avg-cpu:  %user    %nice    %sys    %idle
           0.40     0.00     1.39   98.21

Device:            tps    Blk_read/s   Blk_wrtn/s   Blk_read   Blk_wrtn
dev3-0           55.16       736.51        60.32       1856        152
dev8-0            0.00         0.00         0.00          0          0
dev8-1         1796.03     14374.60         0.00      36224          0
```

This listing shows that device 8-1, the ATA drive array, is doing the majority of the work in the system. CPU time is registering as 98% idle, so this might lead an observer to think that the system was idling along without much stress; however, a look at the top command shows the error in this assumption:. The output of the top command for the same time period is shown below:

```
21:01:35  up 14 days,  3:32,  1 user,   load average: 2.00, 2.00, 2.00
65 processes: 64 sleeping, 1 running, 0 zombie, 0 stopped
CPU states:  cpu     user    nice   system    irq  softirq  iowait    idle
            total     0.4%    0.0%    0.0%    0.4%    0.0%   49.5%   49.5%
            cpu00     0.0%    0.0%    0.0%    0.9%    0.0%    0.0%   99.0%
            cpu01     0.9%    0.0%    0.0%    0.0%    0.0%   99.0%    0.0%
```

```
Mem:   4067556k av,  4048420k used,    19136k free,        0k shrd,   281432k buff
                     3063424k actv,   798872k in_d,    20108k in_c
Swap: 2040244k av,    577540k used,  1462704k free      3555660k cached
```

This listing shows just the header from an I/O stat taken during
the ATA query runs. The system is 98% idle with the CPU
because it is 100% I/O bound on the processor that is handling
the I/O for the query. The VMSTAT command also confirms
this as is shown below:

```
procs                     memory      swap         io    system         cpu
 r  b   swpd   free   buff  cache   si   so   bi   bo   in   cs us sy id wa
 1  1 574436  18864 281432 3557252   13    1   17    7   16    2  3  2  1  6
 0  2 575580  18608 281432 3557580  142   61 3770   82  628  811  1  4 46 49
 1  2 575164  18736 281432 3557728  167  311 3808  337  638  843  0  1 50 49
 0  2 574740  19496 281432 3556400  188    0 3923   16  639  838  0  1 50 49
 1  1 577084  18724 281432 3557972  195  118 3684  142  615  797  0  1 50 50
 2  0 576552  18752 281432 3557452  223    0 3487   36  588  773  0  5 48 47
 0  2 577120  19048 281432 3557268  234   34 3763   48  621  809  0  0 49 51
 1  1 576584  18704 281432 3557072  243  430 3638  454  605  775  1  1 50 49
 0  2 576124  18772 281432 3556524  202  184 3682  210  614  795  1  1 49 49
 1  1 575896  19372 281432 3558408  169  120 3769  134  622  820  0  1 49 49
```

Of course, the I/O timing data from inside Oracle is also a
critical component of the analysis. The script below shows an
example query that can be used to get the I/O timing data for the
various data and temp files:

🖫 IO_timing

```
-- ***********************************************************
-- Copyright © 2005 by Rampant TechPress
-- This script is free for non-commercial purposes
-- with no warranties.  Use at your own risk.
--
-- To license this script for a commercial purpose,
-- contact info@rampant.cc
-- ***********************************************************

Col file# format 99999 heading 'File#'
col name format a45 heading 'Name'
col phywrts heading 'Phys.|Writes'
col phyrds heading 'Phys.|Reads'
col read_rat heading 'Avg.|Read|Time' format 990.000
col write_rat heading 'Avg.|Write|Time' format 990.000
set lines 132 pages 45
ttitle 'I/O Timing Analysis'
spool io_time
select  f.FILE# ,d.name,PHYRDS,PHYWRTS,READTIM/greatest(PHYRDS,1)
read_rat,WRITETIM/greatest(PHYWRTS,1) write_rat
from v$filestat f, v$datafile d
where f.file#=d.file#
union
```

```
select  f.FILE# ,d.name,PHYRDS,PHYWRTS,READTIM/greatest(PHYRDS,1)
read_rat,WRITETIM/greatest(PHYWRTS,1) write_rat
from v$tempstat f, v$tempfile d
where f.file#=d.file#
order by 5 desc;
spool off
ttitle off
clear columns
set lines 80 pages 22
```

The script queries the *v$tempfile* and *v$datafile* views for timing data and shows the average time per I/O operation on the files. An example report is shown below:

```
Mon Jul 19                                               page    1
                           I/O Timing Analysis
                                                         Avg.    Avg.
                                          Phys.  Phys.   Read    Write
File# Name                                Reads  Writes  Time    Time
----- --------------------------------  -------- ------- ------- -------
    3 /u12/oracle/oradata/dss/undotbs103.dbf     50    397  1.400  0.073
   13 /u10/oracle/oradata/dss/xdb01.dbf          11      3  1.363  0.333
    1 /u08/oracle/oradata/dss/system01.dbf    12857   1201  1.127  0.087
    4 /u11/oracle/oradata/dss/undotbs102.dbf    313   3157  0.785  0.069
    2 /u09/oracle/oradata/dss/undotbs101.dbf     50   2979  0.760  0.064
    2 /u12/oracle/oradata/dss/tem102.dbf          4      0  0.500  0.000
    1 /u12/oracle/oradata/dss/tem101.dbf       8733  25480  0.480  0.599
    5 /u08/oracle/oradata/dss/dss_data01.dbf 33688717    3  0.448  0.000
    7 /u10/oracle/oradata/dss/dss_data03.dbf 30345274    3  0.444  0.000
    6 /u09/oracle/oradata/dss/dss_data02.dbf 29910924    3  0.441  0.000
   11 /u09/oracle/oradata/dss/drsys01.dbf         5      3  0.400  0.333
    3 /u12/oracle/oradata/dss/temp05.dbf          4      0  0.250  0.000
   12 /u09/oracle/oradata/dss/tools01.dbf         5      3  0.200  0.000
   15 /u10/oracle/oradata/dss_index05.dbf         5      3  0.200  0.000
   16 /u09/oracle/oradata/dss_index06.dbf         5      3  0.200  0.000
   17 /u08/oracle/oradata/dss_index07.dbf         5      3  0.200  0.000
   10 /u14/oracle/oradata/dss/dss_index03.dbf 173160    3  0.110  0.000
    9 /u13/oracle/oradata/dss_index02.dbf    181979      3  0.106  0.000
    8 /u11/oracle/oradata/dss_index01.dbf    182678      3  0.102  0.333
   14 /u13/oracle/oradata/dss/dss_index3.dbf  11554      3  0.017  0.000
    4 /u01/oracle/oradata/dss/temp021.dbf         0      0  0.000  0.000
    5 /u02/oracle/oradata/dss/temp022.dbf         0      0  0.000  0.000
   18 /u03/oracle/oradata/dss/undo021.dbf         0      3  0.000  0.000
   19 /u04/oracle/oradata/dss/uno022.dbf          0      3  0.000  0.000

24 rows selected.
```

It is apparent that the I/O times are actually quite acceptable for a disk I/O subsystem. All I/O times for the filesystems of concern are fractional milliseconds. However, when the volume of I/O operations is large, even a fractional time multiplies rapidly. In this case, moving to SSD assets is indicated.

So far the use of scripts to determine I/O rates and timings has been covered. From this data, the files that are experiencing the most I/O should be placed on the SSD drive. However, this is not the total picture. It is also necessary to look at the wait interface to see if the I/O is actually generating wait related issues. While self generated scripts can be used, the STATSPACK scripts do a great job on reporting against the wait interface.

Using the STATSPACK Report to Analyze I/O Performance

The STATSPACK utility has shipped with every Oracle Database since version 8.1.7.2. This commonality makes it a logical choice for analyzing databases for use with SSD. STATSPACK provides a plethora of I/O related statistics as well all the needed wait interface statistics.

Installing STATSPACK

Installation of STATSPACK is actually quite simple:

- Create a tablespace in which to store the captured STATSPACK statistics. Usually 100-500 Megabytes is enough, but one should certainly set aside 500 Megabytes if STATSPACK is to be used on a continuing basis. This tablespace is normally called *perfstat*.

- From the *sys* user, the *statspack* user, table, and packaged creation script should be run. Usually this is: *$ORACLE_HOME/rdbms/admin/spcreate.sq;* however, this may be different on older Oracle releases.

- Log in as the *perfstat* user and execute the *statspack.snap* procedure.

- Following a reasonable collection interval, the *statspack.snap* procedure should be re-run.

- From the *perfstat* user, the STATSPACK reporting script: *$ORACLE_HOME/rdbms/admin/spreport*, should be run for the interval over which statistics were just collected.

Reviewing the STATSPACK Report for SSD

The STATSPACK report can run to dozens of pages depending on the number of files, amount of SQL generated, and a number of other parameters. However, in determining what files should be placed on SSD assets, the most important section of the report is the one dealing with the wait interface. On the first page of the report, the top five wait events are shown. The listing below shows the STATSPACK report for a run with the data files on the ATA drives.

```
Top 5 Timed Events
~~~~~~~~~~~~~~~~~~~                                            % Total
Event                             Waits       Time (s)  Ela Time
-------------------------------   ------------  -----------  --------
db file sequential read            93,211,687     398,236     96.80
CPU time                                          10,892      2.65
db file scattered read                344,252       1,512       .37
control file parallel write           141,759         583       .14
latch free                              8,947          90       .02
                                  ------------------------------------
```

For those not familiar with the various waits captured by the wait interface, Table 5.1 shows the major I/O related waits:

WAIT EVENT	DESCRIPTION
Datafile I/O-Related Wait Events:	
db file sequential read	Wait for single block read of a table or index
db file scattered read	Wait for Multi-block read of a table or index (full scan)
db file parallel read	Used when Oracle performs in parallel reads from multiple datafiles to non-contiguous buffers in memory (PGA or Buffer Cache). Similar to db file sequential read

WAIT EVENT	DESCRIPTION
direct path read	Used by Oracle when reading directly into PGA (sort or hash)
direct path write	Used by Oracle when writing directly into PGA (sort or hash)
direct path read (lob)	Read of a LOB segment
direct path write (lob)	Write of a LOB segment
Controlfile I/O-Related Wait Events:	
control file parallel write	Waiting for the writes of CF records to the CF files
control file sequential read	Occurs on I/O to a single copy of the controlfile
control file single write	Occurs on I/O to a single copy of the controlfile
Redo Logging I/O-Related Wait Events:	
log file parallel write	Waiting for the writes of redo records to the redo log files
log file sync	User session waits on this wait event while waiting for LGWR to post after commit write of dirty blocks
log file sequential read	LGWR background process waits for this event while it is copying redo records from the memory Log Buffer cache to the current redo group's member logfiles on disk.
log file single write	This Wait Event is I/O-related so it is likely to appear together with 'log file parallel write'
switch logfile command	Wait cause by manual redo log switch command
log file switch completion	Wait generated while buffers are written during log switch
log file switch (clearing log file)	Wait generated while buffers are written during log switch
log file switch (checkpoint incomplete)	Wait generated while buffers are written during log switch, only for when checkpoint takes longer than normal
log switch/archive	Wait generated while buffers are written during log switch

Analyzing What to Put On SSD **127**

WAIT EVENT	DESCRIPTION
log file switch (archiving needed)	Wait generated while buffers are written during log switch, only for when cannot write immediately to archive log location

Table 5.1: *I/O Related Wait Events*

The *db file sequential read* wait event dominates the events display in Top Five Timed Event output above. From Table 5.1, this is due to single block reads of indexes or tables. With nearly 97% of non-idle wait time, this is clearly what needs to be examined.

By looking at the listing below, where the results from a STATSPACK taken with the data files on the SSD drives are shown, one can see that if only the data files are moved to the SSD asset, there will be a 93% drop, from 398,236 to 31,030, in I/O related wait time for the same queries even though actual waits remained virtually unchanged. CPU time has also dropped to 30% of its previous value.

Moving the data files was predicated by review of the I/O rate information from previous listings correlated with the I/O waits seen in the STATSPACK listing.

```
Top 5 Timed Events
~~~~~~~~~~~~~~~~~~~                                        % Total
Event                              Waits    Time (s) Ela Time
-----------------------------  ------------ ----------- --------
db file sequential read          99,991,232      31,030    88.65
CPU time                                          3,343     9.55
control file parallel write          19,300         375     1.07
db file scattered read              174,949         157      .45
control file sequential read          7,764          50      .14
                               -------------------------------------------
```

Another section of the STATSPACK report which must be utilized for determining I/O characteristics is the data file I/O section. The listing below shows the I/O section of the STATSPACK report:

```
Tablespace              Filename
--------------------    ------------------------------------------------
                 Av     Av    Av                          Av     Buffer Av Buf
         Reads Reads/s Rd(ms) Blks/Rd       Writes Writes/s     Waits Wt(ms)
------------- ------- ------ ------------ ------------- --------- ---------- ------
DSS_DATA                /u08/oracle/oradata/dss/dss_data01.dbf
    33,299,194     76   4.4    1.1            0         0          0
                        /u09/oracle/oradata/dss/dss_data02.dbf
    29,693,254     68   4.3    1.1            0         0          0
                        /u10/oracle/oradata/dss/dss_data03.dbf
    30,079,180     69   4.4    1.1            0         0          0
DSS_INDEX               /u11/oracle/oradata/dss/dss_index01.dbf
       159,622      0   6.2    1.0            0         0          0
                        /u13/oracle/oradata/dss/dss_index02.dbf
       151,677      0   7.2    1.0            0         0          0
                        /u13/oracle/oradata/dss/dss_index3.dbf
        11,549      0   0.1    1.0            0         0          0
                        /u14/oracle/oradata/dss/dss_index03.dbf
       149,736      0   7.3    1.0            0         0          0
PERFSTAT                /u05/oracle/oradata/dss/perfstat1.dbf
            10      0   2.0    1.5          172         0          0
SYSTEM                  /u08/oracle/oradata/dss/system01.dbf
        11,375      0  12.6    4.0          998         0          0
TEMP2                   /u01/oracle/oradata/dss/temp021.dbf
       138,030      0   0.3    3.4       46,979         0          0
                        /u02/oracle/oradata/dss/temp022.dbf
       139,933      0   0.2    2.3       33,505         0          0
UNDO2                   /u03/oracle/oradata/dss/undo021.dbf
            56      0   4.5    1.0        4,162         0         17   30.6
                        /u04/oracle/oradata/dss/uno022.dbf
           116      0   2.6    1.0        1,241         0          0
          -------------------------------------------------------------
```

From this listing, one can see that the data files are seeing the majority of the I/O stress showing the most I/O per second and high read times. Once the data files are moved to the SSD drive, these values change dramatically as shown by the listing below:

```
File I/O Stats for DB: DSS  Instance: dss  Snaps: 1 -2
->ordered by Tablespace, File
Tablespace              Filename
--------------------    ------------------------------------------------
                 Av     Av    Av                          Av     Buffer Av Buf
         Reads Reads/s Rd(ms) Blks/Rd       Writes Writes/s     Waits Wt(ms)
------------- ------- ------ ------------ ------------- --------- ---------- ------
DSS_DATA                /u01/oracle/oradata/dss/dss_data01.dbf
    35,975,161    602   0.3    1.0            0         0          0
                        /u02/oracle/oradata/dss/dss_data02.dbf
    31,756,793    532   0.3    1.0            0         0          0
                        /u03/oracle/oradata/dss/dss_data03.dbf
    32,279,053    540   0.3    1.0            0         0          0
DSS_INDEX               /u11/oracle/oradata/dss/dss_index01.dbf
        46,863      1   0.3    1.0            0         0          0
                        /u13/oracle/oradata/dss/dss_index02.dbf
        50,032      1   0.3    1.0            0         0          0
                        /u14/oracle/oradata/dss/dss_index03.dbf
        49,166      1   0.3    1.0            0         0          0
PERFSTAT                /u12/oracle/oradata/dss/perfstat.dbf
            37      0  18.6    1.0           92         0          0
SYSTEM                  /u08/oracle/oradata/dss/system01.dbf
         5,358      0   4.3    2.0        1,549         0          0
TEMP                    /u12/oracle/oradata/dss/temp011.dbf
       113,460      2   4.5    2.7       35,450         1          0
UNDOTBS                 /u08/oracle/oradata/dss/undo01.dbf
         1,626      0   2.7    1.0        2,138         0          1   60.0
                        /u09/oracle/oradata/dss/undo02.dbf
           537      0   3.4    1.0          631         0          0
          -------------------------------------------------------------
```

I/O per second has increased by a factor of five to six times, while the average read time has dropped from four to five milliseconds to less than a millisecond. This difference is reflected in the query times reported for earlier runs.

As a matter of conjecture, moving data to the SSD and then dropping selected indexes could actually improve performance by eliminating slow index I/O, assuming they are on SCSI or ATA disks, and moving that I/O instead to faster SSD full table scans.

Based on this analysis, moving the data and index tablespaces would give the best results since the highest stress is on the data and index datafiles based on I/O readings and on the waits. *db_file_scattered_reads* are full table or full index scans, and *db_file_sequential_reads* are single point reads of tables or indexes. In tests where the undo and temporary tablespaces where moved to the SSD array for this database, there were no appreciable gains in performance.

However, if the majority or a significant percentage of the waits shown were due to undo segments or temporary tablespace related activity, such as sort and hash related waits or direct I/O related waits, moving them to the SSD asset would make sense.

The most important fact to remember about moving files to the SSD asset is that the only gain in performance will be the percentage of time spent waiting on that asset. If the amount waited on for a temporary tablespace is less than one percent of the total application wait time, moving the temporary tablespace to the SSD can only gain a maximum of one percent in performance.

In the example presented so far, the physical I/O in the system, most of which was directed at the data tablespace datafiles, was causing the significant amount of system wait time, so by moving the data tablespace datafiles, there were significant gains in performance.

If there was sufficient room on the SSD asset, moving the index tablespace data files would be the next logical move.

The following listing shows the timing related part of the header from another systems STATSPACK report:

```
             Snap Id     Snap Time      Sessions Curs/Sess Comment
             -------  ------------------ -------- --------- ----- --
Begin Snap:      11 27-Oct-03 12:00:05      19       3.4
  End Snap:      19 27-Oct-03 20:00:03      14       3.3
  Elapsed:               479.97 (mins)
```

The time span is long enough to guarantee a good sample. Users need to be sure that the STATSPACK used is not just for a specific transaction but covers a period of normal activity in the database. The following listing shows the resulting wait profile:

```
Top 5 Timed Events
~~~~~~~~~~~~~~~~~~~                                      % Total
Event                                         Waits   Ela Time
------------------------------------------- ------------ --------
control file parallel write                    9,306      30.15
db file scattered read                        34,516      19.27
db file sequential read                       86,156      18.18
SQL*Net message from dblink                   15,882      13.99
CPU time                                                  12.42
------------------------------------------------------------
```

I/O related waits dominate this listing. In this listing, it is odd that *control file parallel writes* are the predominant wait activity. This is in no doubt due to their being collocated with the other database files. Logic would seem to indicate that moving the control files to SSD assets would be the best course of action. However, they are usually low I/O files and if they were moved to another disk asset, their wait contribution would probably disappear. This leaves the data and index related I/O and reflects a need to look at the I/O profile for the database. The following listing shows an excerpt from the I/O section of the same report showing all datafiles with I/O greater than 500.

```
File I/O Stats for DB: TSTPROD  Instance: TSTprod  Snaps: 11 -19
->ordered by Tablespace, File

Tablespace             Filename
---------------------- ---------------------------------------------------
                   Av   Av    Av                     Av      Buffer Av Buf
           Reads Reads/s Rd(ms) Blks/Rd   Writes Writes/s   Waits Wt(ms)
-------------- ------- ------- ------- ------- ----------- -------- -------- ---------- ------
NAME_ADDRESS_JUNCTION_XI G:\ORADATA\GLOBAL_NAMES\INDEXES\NAME_ADDRESS_JUNCTIO
           502      0    6.2    1.0       218       0        0
NAME_ADDRESS_JUNCTION_XI G:\ORADATA\GLOBAL_NAMES\INDEXES\NAME_ADDRESS_JUNCTIO
           332      0    6.8    1.0       425       0        0
NAME_ADDRESS_JUNCTION_XU G:\ORADATA\GLOBAL_NAMES\INDEXES\NAME_ADDRESS_JUNCTIO
           797      0    6.3    1.0       637       0        0
NAME_ADDRESS_TBL         F:\ORADATA\GLOBAL_NAMES\TABLES\NAME_ADDRESS_TBL.DBF
           480      0    9.0    1.0       496       0        0
NAME_ADDRESS_XID         G:\ORADATA\GLOBAL_NAMES\INDEXES\NAME_ADDRESS_XID.DBF
         2,131      0    7.3    1.0     2,334       0        0
NAME_TBL                 F:\ORADATA\GLOBAL_NAMES\TABLES\NAME_TBL.DBF
           489      0    7.1    1.0       189       0        0
NAME_XID                 G:\ORADATA\GLOBAL_NAMES\INDEXES\NAME_XID.DBF
           574      0    8.1    1.0       733       0        0
RBS                      H:\ORADATA\GLOBAL_NAMES\RBS1.DBF
             5      0    0.0    1.0     2,198       0        0
SMALL_TBL                F:\ORADATA\GLOBAL_NAMES\TABLES\SMALL_TBL.DBF
        36,288      1    3.4   14.3        15       0       44    2.3
SYSTEM                   H:\ORADATA\GLOBAL_NAMES\SYSTEM01.DBF
        75,856      3    0.8    1.0       164       0        0
TOOLS                    D:\ORACLE\ORADATA\GLOBAL_NAMES\TOOLS01.DBF
           474      0    4.6    1.0     1,076       0        0
USERS                    D:\ORACLE\ORADATA\GLOBAL_NAMES\USERS01.DBF
           423      0    6.1    4.8       415       0        0
XDB                      D:\ORACLE\ORADATA\GLOBAL_NAMES\XDB01.DBF
           603      0    2.9    1.0         0       0        0
```

From the I/O profile in this listing, moving *small_tbl* or *system* would yield the biggest gain followed by moving *name_address_xid* and then *RBS*. However, anytime I/O to SYSTEM is as excessive as it is in this case, its causes should be determined and eliminated.

Using AWRRPT Reports

Introduced in Oracle10g, the AWRRPT report replaces the STATSPACK reports in previous releases. One note of caution is that specific licenses are required for the use of the AWRRPT, just as with any of the other new tuning features in 10g. The STATSPACK reports are still available in 10g and are still cost free, so they can continue to be used.

The AWRRPT report comes in two flavors, the text based and the HTML based versions. To post results to a web page, or if the fancy format is appealing, the HTML version is the one to use. Anyone who likes the look and feel of the old STATSPACK will still be able to rely upon the text based version. To generate the either the HTML or text version, the *$ORACLE_HOME/rdbms/admin/awrrpt.sql* script can be used, and it will prompt for the appropriate version of the report to generate.

The header from the AWRRPT output looks nearly identical to that from the STATSPACK reports as shown in the listing report. A complete sample AWRRPT report is shown in Appendix B.

```
WORKLOAD REPOSITORY report for

DB Name        DB Id      Instance     Inst Num Release     Cluster Host
------------ ----------- ------------- -------- ----------- ------- -----------
SSD           534227347 ssd2                  2 10.1.0.3.0  YES
amd44.supers

                 Snap Id      Snap Time       Sessions Curs/Sess
                 --------- ------------------- -------- ---------
Begin Snap:          3 28-Jul-05 18:59:48       124      14.4
  End Snap:          4 28-Jul-05 20:00:19       106        .7
  Elapsed:              60.52 (mins)
  DB Time:               9.87 (mins)

Cache Sizes (end)
~~~~~~~~~~~~~~~~~
           Buffer Cache:         768M     Std Block Size:         8K
       Shared Pool Size:         244M         Log Buffer:       512K

Load Profile
~~~~~~~~~~~~                     Per Second       Per Transaction
                              ---------------     ---------------
           Redo size:          14,614.81             7,031.32
       Logical reads:           1,690.46               813.30
       Block changes:              81.77                39.34
       Physical reads:              1.52                 0.73
      Physical writes:             12.73                 6.12
           User calls:              8.15                 3.92
               Parses:              1.40                 0.68
          Hard parses:              0.00                 0.00
                Sorts:              0.59                 0.28
               Logons:              0.03                 0.02
             Executes:             19.37                 9.32
         Transactions:              2.08

% Blocks changed per Read:   4.84   Recursive Call %:    75.25
Rollback per transaction %:  2.08     Rows per Sort:      9.38
```

```
Instance Efficiency Percentages (Target 100%)
~~~~~~~~~~~~~~~~~~~~~~~~~~~~~~~~~~~~~~~~~~~~~~~~
            Buffer Nowait %:   99.97    Redo NoWait %:   99.98
            Buffer  Hit   %:   99.91    In-memory Sort %: 100.00
            Library Hit   %:   99.99      Soft Parse %:   99.86
          Execute to Parse %:  92.76      Latch Hit %:    99.98
Parse CPU to Parse Elapsd %:  104.48   % Non-Parse CPU:   99.66

Shared Pool Statistics        Begin    End
                              ------   ------
            Memory Usage %:   37.87    38.16
     % SQL with executions>1: 84.98    86.15
     % Memory for SQL w/exec>1: 77.84  80.07

Top 5 Timed Events
~~~~~~~~~~~~~~~~~~~                                  % Total
Event                                               DB Time    Wait
Class                         Waits    Time (s)
------------------------------ ----------- ----------- --------- -------------
enq: TX - row lock contention     596         208      35.17
Application
CPU time                                      204      34.39
gc cr block 2-way              49,722          77      13.00
Cluster
gc current block 2-way         36,791          52       8.74
Cluster
gc buffer busy                  1,726          29       4.86
Cluster
------------------------------------------------------------------
```

About the only item changed in the heading for the AWRRPT report from the STATSPACK report is that the Top 5 Timed Event section reports are based on the percentage of total DB time and reports the Wait Class. It appears that some of the statistics reported may be suspect or mislabeled. For example, on some of the reports examined during testing, the value for *% Non-Parse CPU* is negative. In earlier versions of STATSPACK, this also occurred, but it was corrected. It appears to have been reborn. Also noted was that in some of the Top 5 Wait Events, *% Total DB Time* is not a percentage but appears to be the actual time. Unfortunately, the code that generates these reports has been internalized so it is difficult to get a good idea of what the developers meant to have in these places.

However, the data is still present to allow users to determine if the system would benefit from being a SSD system or not. One thing to note in the header is the amount of time spent doing I/O versus doing CPU related work. In the above header listing, non-I/O related events are displayed. All of the events, other than the TX enqueue and CPU values, are RAC interconnect

Oracle RAC & Grid Tuning with SSD

related. This report was taken during one of the fully cached data runs.

If the report is run on a RAC environment, the section immediately following the heading is for RAC related statistics. The listing below shows an example from the same test run as the last listing above.

```
RAC Statistics  DB/Inst: SSD/ssd2  Snaps: 3-4
                               Begin   End
                               -----  -----
            Number of Instances:   2     2

Global Cache Load Profile
~~~~~~~~~~~~~~~~~~~~~~~~~~              Per Second      Per Transaction
                                       ---------------  ---------------
     Global Cache blocks received:          25.46            12.25
       Global Cache blocks served:          30.66            14.75
       GCS/GES messages received:           45.19            21.74
            GCS/GES messages sent:          41.24            19.84
               DBWR Fusion writes:           2.61             1.25

Global Cache Efficiency Percentages (Target local+remote 100%)
~~~~~~~~~~~~~~~~~~~~~~~~~~~~~~~~~~~~~~~~~~~~~~~~~~~~~~~~~~~~~~~~~~
Buffer access -  local cache %:  98.40
Buffer access - remote cache %:   1.51
Buffer access -         disk %:   0.09

Global Cache and Enqueue Services - Workload Characteristics
~~~~~~~~~~~~~~~~~~~~~~~~~~~~~~~~~~~~~~~~~~~~~~~~~~~~~~~~~~~~~~~~~~
                  Avg global enqueue get time (ms):   5.5

         Avg global cache cr block receive time (ms):   1.6
    Avg global cache current block receive time (ms):   1.7
           Avg global cache cr block build time (ms):   0.0
            Avg global cache cr block send time (ms):   0.0
    Global cache log flushes for cr blocks served %:   4.2
           Avg global cache cr block flush time (ms):   0.6
       Avg global cache current block pin time (ms):   0.2
      Avg global cache current block send time (ms):   0.0
 Global cache log flushes for current blocks served %:   0.5
     Avg global cache current block flush time (ms):  21.9

Global Cache and Enqueue Services - Messaging Statistics
~~~~~~~~~~~~~~~~~~~~~~~~~~~~~~~~~~~~~~~~~~~~~~~~~~~~~~~~~~~~
                 Avg message sent queue time (ms):   0.0
         Avg message sent queue time on ksxp (ms):   0.6
            Avg message received queue time (ms):   0.0
            Avg GCS message process time (ms):   0.1
            Avg GES message process time (ms):   0.0

                % of direct sent messages:  72.39
               % of indirect sent messages:  26.84
              % of flow controlled messages:   0.77
--------------------------------------------------------------
```

The RAC summary listing shown above gives summarized data about cache transfers and other RAC related statistics. It is likely that the most important statistics related to making a determination about use of SSD are the statistics relating to the

Global Cache Service (GCS). The GCS performs the transfer of blocks between the instances. From looking at this section, one can see that the transfer times for the RAC cluster are in the range of one to two milliseconds for the transfer of blocks. This essentially says that as long as read and write times from the SSD device are faster than the interconnect block transfer time, it is prudent to push processing away from the interconnect and to the SSD.

The next section covers the foreground wait event section. This section shows all of the *instance wait* events and the Top 5 Wait Events section is a subset of these values. The report in the following listing has been truncated to only show the first 20 readings. The normal report runs to nearly two and one half pages of data. Oracle tries to push the *idle wait* events to the bottom of the listing.

```
Wait Events  DB/Inst: SSD/ssd2  Snaps: 3-4
-> s  - second
-> cs - centisecond -     100th of a second
-> ms - millisecond -    1000th of a second
-> us - microsecond - 1000000th of a second
-> ordered by wait time desc, waits desc (idle events last)
```

Event	Waits	Timeouts	Total Wait Time (s)	Avg wait (ms)	Waits /txn
enq: TX - row lock contenti	596	324	208	349	0.1
gc cr block 2-way	49,722	0	77	2	6.6
gc current block 2-way	36,791	0	52	1	4.9
gc buffer busy	1,726	2	29	17	0.2
SQL*Net more data from clie	830	0	26	32	0.1
latch: library cache lock	96	0	26	271	0.0
latch: cache buffers chains	1,043	1,018	13	12	0.1
gc current block busy	275	0	10	37	0.0
class slave wait	2	2	10	4995	0.0
gc cr block busy	2,599	0	6	2	0.3
gc cr multi block request	3,096	0	3	1	0.4
enq: TX - allocate ITL entr	8	5	3	362	0.0
gc current grant busy	7,525	0	3	0	1.0
log file parallel write	10,410	0	2	0	1.4
log file sync	6,756	0	2	0	0.9
db file sequential read	5,500	0	2	0	0.7
buffer busy waits	110	0	2	16	0.0
gcs log flush sync	2,674	104	2	1	0.4
control file parallel write	1,498	0	1	1	0.2
gc current grant 2-way	2,530	0	1	1	0.3

The events in the *Foreground Event* report are those that occurred in user or application processes. If excessive GCS type events

Oracle RAC & Grid Tuning with SSD

dominate the report, the interconnect is causing most of the *wait events* in the database. Likewise, if I/O related events such as *db file scattered read* or *db file sequential read* dominate, the system is becoming I/O bound. Both interconnect issues and I/O bound conditions can be fixed quickly using SSD. The next section of the report deals with the background *wait events*. These are *wait events* from the Oracle background processes such as SMON, PMON or DBWR. The following listing shows an example of this section of the AWRRPT report.

```
Background Wait Events  DB/Inst: SSD/ssd2  Snaps: 3 4
-> ordered by wait time desc, waits desc (idle events last)

                                                          Avg
                                             Total Wait  wait   Waits
Event                      Waits   Timeouts  Time (s)    (ms)   /txn
------------------------- -------- --------- ---------- ------- --------
log file parallel write    10,411         0          2       0    1.4
gcs log flush sync          2,674       104          2       1    0.4
control file parallel write 1,496         0          1       1    0.2
control file sequential rea 4,507         0          1       0    0.6
process startup                14         0          1      39    0.0
DFS lock handle             2,172         0          0       0    0.3
CGS wait for IPC msg       31,913    31,913          0       0    4.2
latch: cache buffers chains    23        23          0       5    0.0
enq: CF - contention          163         0          0       1    0.0
gc cr block 2-way              66         0          0       1    0.0
gc current block 2-way         55         0          0       1    0.0
enq: HW - contention          161         0          0       0    0.0
latch: KCL gc element paren    13        11          0       3    0.0
db file parallel write     26,742         0          0       0    3.5
control file single write     100         0          0       0    0.0
row cache lock                 44         0          0       0    0.0
ksxr poll remote instances  2,843     2,650          0       0    0.4
IPC send completion sync       15        15          0       1    0.0
reliable message               27         0          0       0    0.0
PX Deq: Signal ACK             35        12          0       0    0.0
           ------------------------------------------------------------
```

Again, this report was cut off at 20 events. The full report can be a page or more in length. Usually, the background *wait event* report is not very useful in tuning unless there are background process issues to diagnose.

The next report section is new in the 10g AWRRPT and not available in STATSPACK. It is the Time Model Statistics report, and it breaks down exactly how the system spent the timeframe for the report. The following listing shows an example from the test runs:

```
Time Model Statistics  DB/Inst: SSD/ssd2  Snaps: 3-4
-> ordered by Time (seconds) desc

                                                   Time      % Total
Statistic Name                                  (seconds)    DB Time
--------------------------------------------  -------------  ---------
DB time                                            592.04     100.00
sql execute elapsed time                           586.23      99.02
DB CPU                                             203.60      34.39
background elapsed time                             45.51       7.69
background cpu time                                 22.46       3.79
PL/SQL execution elapsed time                        1.63        .28
connection management call elapsed time              1.30        .22
parse time elapsed                                    .58        .10
sequence load elapsed time                            .02        .00
hard parse (sharing criteria) elapsed time            .00        .00
hard parse (bind mismatch) elapsed time               .00        .00
hard parse elapsed time                               .00        .00
Java execution elapsed time                           .00        .00
failed parse elapsed time                             .00        .00
PL/SQL compilation elapsed time                       .00        .00
inbound PL/SQL rpc elapsed time                       .00        .00
failed parse (out of shared memory) elapsed t         .00        .00
                                              -----------------------------------

Operating System Statistics  DB/Inst: SSD/ssd2  Snaps: 3-4

Statistic Name                                 Value
-----------------------------------  ------------------
AVG_BUSY_TICKS                                11,641
AVG_IDLE_TICKS                               349,688
AVG_IN_BYTES                             851,628,032
AVG_NICE_TICKS                                     0
AVG_OUT_BYTES                          1,107,304,448
AVG_SYS_TICKS                                  2,335
AVG_USER_TICKS                                 9,306
BUSY_TICKS                                    23,282
IDLE_TICKS                                   699,377
IN_BYTES                               1,703,256,064
NICE_TICKS                                         0
OUT_BYTES                              2,214,608,896
RSRC_MGR_CPU_WAIT_TIME                             0
SYS_TICKS                                      4,670
USER_TICKS                                    18,612
                                     ------------------------------------------
```

Between the supplied Oracle internal statistics and the system time ticks values, one can quickly determine how the system spent its time for the report interval. In the example report, the time was spent running SQL. This example was for a 2-CPU system, so the total time calculates out to 200% rather than 100%.

The next section of the AWRRPT report is also new in 10g. It reports on the various services and shows their activity levels. The following listing is an example from the report:

```
Service Statistics  DB/Inst: SSD/ssd2  Snaps: 3-4
-> ordered by DB Time

                                           Physical   Logical
Service Name      DB Time (s)  DB CPU (s)     Reads      Reads
----------------  -----------  ----------  ---------- ----------
ssd                     591.9       203.5      5,468  6,041,482
SYS$USERS                 0.1         0.1          0         36
SYS$BACKGROUND            0.0         0.0         52     96,198
ssdXDB                    0.0         0.0          0          0
                  ---------------------------------------------------------

Service Wait Class Stats  DB/Inst: SSD/ssd2  Snaps: 3-4
-> Wait Class info for services in the Service Statistics section.
-> Total Waits and Time Waited displayed for the following wait
   classes:  User I/O, Concurrency, Administrative, Network
-> Time Waited (Wt Time) in centisecond (100th of a second)

Service Name
--------------------------------------------------------------------
 User I/O  User I/O  Concurcy Concurcy    Admin    Admin   Network Network
Total Wts  Wt Time Total Wts  Wt Time Total Wts  Wt Time Total Wts Wt Time
---------  ------- --------- -------- --------- ------- --------- -------
ssd
     7806      242      1411     4114         0        0     31702    2628
SYS$USERS
        0        0         0        0         0        0        72       0
SYS$BACKGROUND
    49003        1       147       16         0        0         1       0
                  ---------------------------------------------------------
```

This report shows exactly which services spent the most time waiting, and in general, what they waited for. Some times are reported in units of centaseconds while others are in seconds. In this report, the SSD service dominates the time utilized. This was the service used to run the test cases. The high percentage of reads that are logical reads indicate a nearly fully cached system.

The next several sections of the full AWRRPT deal with SQL code; however, since this book is not about SQL tuning, these sections will be skipped. The next section of interest is the Instance Activity section, which reports the statistics from the *v$sysstat* view. The following listing shows an excerpt from this section of the report highlighting some statistics of interest.

```
Instance Activity Stats  DB/Inst: SSD/ssd2  Snaps: 3-4

Statistic                             Total    per Second   per Trans
-----------------------------  ----------------  ------------  ------------
CPU used by this session              16,669           4.6         2.2
CPU used when call started            16,672           4.6         2.2
DB time                               60,701          16.7         8.0
DBWR checkpoints                           6           0.0         0.0
DBWR fusion writes                     9,462           2.6         1.3
IPC CPU used by this session           1,584           0.4         0.2
consistent changes                    14,651           4.0         1.9
```

consistent gets	5,937,893	1,635.4	786.8
consistent gets - examination	634,674	174.8	84.1
consistent gets from cache	5,937,893	1,635.4	786.8
data blocks consistent reads - u	13,121	3.6	1.7
db block changes	296,900	81.8	39.3
db block gets	200,058	55.1	26.5
db block gets direct	8	0.0	0.0
db block gets from cache	200,050	55.1	26.5
deferred (CURRENT) block cleanou	40,205	11.1	5.3
execute count	70,345	19.4	9.3
free buffer inspected	96,695	26.6	12.8
free buffer requested	109,016	30.0	14.4
gc CPU used by this session	2,264	0.6	0.3
gc cr block build time	142	0.0	0.0
gc cr block flush time	178	0.1	0.0
gc cr block receive time	9,029	2.5	1.2
gc cr block send time	295	0.1	0.0
gc cr blocks received	55,074	15.2	7.3
gc cr blocks served	69,564	19.2	9.2
gc current block flush time	473	0.1	0.1
gc current block pin time	642	0.2	0.1
gc current block receive time	6,463	1.8	0.9
gc current block send time	179	0.1	0.0
gc current blocks received	37,381	10.3	5.0
gc current blocks served	41,766	11.5	5.5
gcs messages sent	142,933	39.4	18.9
ges messages sent	6,809	1.9	0.9
global enqueue CPU used by this	235	0.1	0.0
global enqueue get time	21,353	5.9	2.8
global enqueue gets async	782	0.2	0.1
global enqueue gets sync	38,370	10.6	5.1
global enqueue releases	37,478	10.3	5.0
index fetch by key	208,656	57.5	27.7
index scans kdiixs1	17,232	4.8	2.3
logons cumulative	117	0.0	0.0
no work - consistent read gets	5,251,099	1,446.2	695.8
opened cursors cumulative	4,955	1.4	0.7
physical read IO requests	5,519	1.5	0.7
physical reads	5,520	1.5	0.7
physical reads cache	5,495	1.5	0.7
physical reads cache prefetch	1	0.0	0.0
physical reads direct	25	0.0	0.0
physical write IO requests	39,359	10.8	5.2
physical writes	46,215	12.7	6.1
physical writes direct	33	0.0	0.0
physical writes from cache	46,182	12.7	6.1
physical writes non checkpoint	26,290	7.2	3.5
recursive cpu usage	4,004	1.1	0.5
redo log space requests	45	0.0	0.0
redo log space wait time	5	0.0	0.0
rollback changes - undo records	832	0.2	0.1
rollbacks only - consistent read	1,193	0.3	0.2
sorts (memory)	2,148	0.6	0.3
sorts (rows)	20,148	5.6	2.7
table fetch by rowid	250,482	69.0	33.2
table fetch continued row	88	0.0	0.0
table scan blocks gotten	5,100,198	1,404.7	675.8
table scan rows gotten	1,043,284,622	287,332.5	38,238.3
table scans (short tables)	3,869	1.1	0.5
transaction rollbacks	169	0.1	0.0
user I/O wait time	261	0.1	0.0
user calls	29,599	8.2	3.9
user commits	7,390	2.0	1.0
user rollbacks	157	0.0	0.0
workarea executions - optimal	4,160	1.2	0.6

An entire chapter could be dedicated to the meanings of each of the above statistics for tuning purposes; however, that is not the focus of this book, so only the applicable part will be highlighted. In the above listing, the detailed sections on Global Cache Service (GCS) and Global Enqueue Service (GES) statistics are of particular interest. These sections deal with RAC and are used to calculate latency information. The detailed statistics in the GCS and GES sections allow the user to not only see what the latency is but also to find out exactly where the latency is occurring. For example, the transfer time for a *gc cr* block is made up of the *gc cr block build time*, the *gc cr block flush time* and the *gs cr block send time*. In this case, the largest percentage of the transfer time is the send time component, which indicates the network was the largest component. For the *gc current block*, The largest component was the pin time indicating that users had to wait for other users to get access to the block.

The next section of the AWRRPT report shows begin/end type Instance activity values that should not be diffed.

```
Instance Activity Stats - Absolute Values  DB/Inst: SSD/ssd2  Snaps: 3-4
-> Statistics with absolute values (should not be diffed)
-> Statistics identified by '(derived)' come from sources other than SYSSTAT

Statistic                            Begin Value      End Value
------------------------------       ---------------  ---------------
logons current                                  124              106
open threads (derived)                            4                4
opened cursors current                        1,787               78
                             ------------------------------------------------
Instance Activity Stats - Thread Activity  DB/Inst: SSD/ssd2  Snaps: 3-4
Statistic                                  Total   per Hour
------------------------------       ------------------  --------
log switches (derived)                          6     5.95
                             ------------------------------------------------
```

The next sections of the report deal with the tablespace and file I/O statistics. In a non-fully cached environment, this section of the report should be reviewed to see what datafiles are undergoing the most I/O. These are prime candidates for a move to SSD resource. The following is an example of this part of the report:

```
Tablespace I/O Stats  DB/Inst: SSD/ssd2  Snaps: 3-4
-> ordered by IOs (Reads + Writes) desc
Tablespace
------------------------------
                  Av     Av    Av                        Av    Buffer Av Buf
          Reads Reads/s Rd(ms) Blks/Rd     Writes Writes/s  Waits Wt(ms)
         ------- ------- ------ ------- ------------ -------- ---------- ------
SSD_DATA
          5,469       2    0.4     1.0       38,133       11      1,306   21.6
UNDOTBS2
              5       0    0.0     1.0          942        0         12    6.7
SYSAUX
             21       0    0.0     1.0          197        0          0    0.0
SYSTEM
             21       0    0.5     1.0           82        0          3    3.3
UNDOTBS1
              5       0    0.0     1.0            5        0        539    4.3
         -------------------------------------------------------------------

File I/O Stats  DB/Inst: SSD/ssd2  Snaps: 3-4
-> ordered by Tablespace, File
Tablespace              Filename
----------------------- -------------------------------------------------
                  Av     Av    Av                        Av    Buffer Av Buf
          Reads Reads/s Rd(ms) Blks/Rd     Writes Writes/s  Waits Wt(ms)
         ------- ------- ------ ------- ------------ -------- ---------- ------
SYSAUX                  /oracle2/oradata/ssd/sysaux01.dbf
             21       0    0.0     1.0          197        0          0    0.0
SYSTEM                  /oracle2/oradata/ssd/system01.dbf
             21       0    0.5     1.0           82        0          3    3.3
UNDOTBS1                /oracle2/oradata/ssd/undotbs01.dbf
              5       0    0.0     1.0            5        0        539    4.3
UNDOTBS2                /oracle2/oradata/ssd/undotbs02.dbf
              5       0    0.0     1.0          942        0         12    6.7
SSD_DATA                /oracle2/oradata/ssd/ssd_data01.dbf
          5,469       2    0.4     1.0       38,133       11      1,306   21.6
         -------------------------------------------------------------------
```

In the above report, I/O is observed even in a fully cached
environment due to INSERT, UPDATE and DELETE activity
forcing cache replacement to occur.

The next section of the AWRRPT report deals with the *db buffer
cache* area. If a system utilizes more than one cache area, such as
multiple blocksizes, RECYCLE, and KEEP, there will be a
section for that information that pertains to the specialized areas.
If the multiple cache features are not being used, only the default
cache will be reported. The following listing shows an example
from the report:

```
Buffer Pool Statistics  DB/Inst: SSD/ssd2  Snaps: 3-4
-> Standard block size Pools D: default,  K: keep,  R: recycle
-> Default Pools for other block sizes: 2k, 4k, 8k, 16k, 32k

                                            Free Writ   Buffer
    Number of Pool   Buffer   Physical Physical Buff Comp   Busy
  P  Buffers Hit%     Gets      Reads   Writes Wait Wait   Waits
  - --------- ---- --------- --------- -------- ---- ----  ------
  D   94,080  100  6,137,790     5,495   46,182    0    0   1,860
      -----------------------------------------------------------
```

```
Instance Recovery Stats  DB/Inst: SSD/ssd2  Snaps: 3-4
-> B: Begin snapshot,  E: End snapshot
```

	Targt MTTR (s)	Estd MTTR (s)	Recovery Estd IOs	Actual Redo Blks	Target Redo Blks	Log File Size Redo Blks	Log Ckpt Timeout Redo Blks	Log Ckpt Interval Redo Blks
B	0	19	3734	9620	18432	18432	27168	
E	0	17	324	2113	18432	18432	29421	

```
Buffer Pool Advisory  DB/Inst: SSD/ssd2  Snap: 4
-> Only rows with estimated physical reads >0 are displayed
-> ordered by Block Size, Buffers For Estimate
```

P	Size for Estimate (M)	Size Factr	Buffers for Estimate	Est Physical Read Factor	Estimated Physical Reads
D	76	.1	9,310	3.81	119,805
D	152	.2	18,620	2.94	92,654
D	228	.3	27,930	2.58	81,054
D	304	.4	37,240	2.42	76,033
D	380	.5	46,550	2.35	73,802
D	456	.6	55,860	2.29	71,892
D	532	.7	65,170	2.22	69,867
D	608	.8	74,480	1.22	38,368
D	684	.9	83,790	1.02	31,944
D	760	1.0	93,100	1.00	31,500
D	768	1.0	94,080	1.00	31,463
D	836	1.1	102,410	0.99	31,056
D	912	1.2	111,720	0.98	30,675
D	988	1.3	121,030	0.97	30,573
D	1,064	1.4	130,340	0.97	30,513
D	1,140	1.5	139,650	0.97	30,453
D	1,216	1.6	148,960	0.97	30,375
D	1,292	1.7	158,270	0.96	30,268
D	1,368	1.8	167,580	0.96	30,181
D	1,444	1.9	176,890	0.96	30,123
D	1,520	2.0	186,200	0.95	30,009

This database has a 100% hit ratio and the advisor report indicates that the physical memory size would have to be nearly doubled to make only a 5% change in I/O. This is expected from a fully cached environment. Physical reads and writes are present in this section since this is an OLTP environment being modeled. Many transactions are doing UPDATE and DELETE type activity, as well as INSERTs which cause cache replacement and flushes. There are also *buffer busy waits,* which were probably caused by enqueue activity associated with transactions needing the same rows.

The next section of the AWRRPT report deals with the Process Global Area (PGA) statistics. The report example is in the following listing:

```
PGA Aggr Summary  DB/Inst: SSD/ssd2  Snaps: 3-4
-> PGA cache hit % - percentage of W/A (WorkArea) data processed only in-
memory

PGA Cache Hit %  W/A MB Processed  Extra W/A MB Read/Written
--------------- ------------------ --------------------------
          100.0              2,887                          0
                -------------------------------------------------------------
```

```
PGA Aggr Target Stats  DB/Inst: SSD/ssd2  Snaps: 3-4
-> B: Begin snap   E: End snap (rows dentified with B or E contain data
   which is absolute i.e. not diffed over the interval)
-> Auto PGA Target - actual workarea memory target
-> W/A PGA Used    - amount of memory used for all Workareas (manual + auto)
-> %PGA W/A Mem    - percentage of PGA memory allocated to workareas
-> %Auto W/A Mem   - percentage of workarea memory controlled by Auto Mem Mgmt
-> %Man W/A Mem    - percentage of workarea memory under manual control
```

	PGA Aggr Target(M)	Auto PGA Target(M)	PGA Mem Alloc(M)	W/A PGA Used(M)	%PGA W/A Mem	%Auto W/A Mem	%Man W/A Mem	Global Mem Bound(K)
B	340	255	148.7	0.0	.0	.0	.0	17,408
E	340	274	89.8	0.0	.0	.0	.0	17,408

```
PGA Aggr Target Histogram  DB/Inst: SSD/ssd2  Snaps: 3-4
-> Optimal Executions are purely in-memory operations
```

Low Optimal	High Optimal	Total Execs	Optimal Execs	1-Pass Execs	M-Pass Execs
2K	4K	761	761	0	0
512K	1024K	3,399	3,399	0	0

```
PGA Memory Advisory  DB/Inst: SSD/ssd2  Snap: 4
-> When using Auto Memory Mgmt, minimally choose a pga_aggregate_target value
   where Estd PGA Overalloc Count is 0
```

PGA Target Est (MB)	Size Factr	W/A MB Processed	Estd Extra W/A MB Read/ Written to Disk	Estd PGA Cache Hit %	Estd PGA Overalloc Count
43	0.1	7,485.9	2,657.9	74.0	80
85	0.3	7,485.9	1,883.5	80.0	50
170	0.5	7,485.9	298.9	96.0	0
255	0.8	7,485.9	298.9	96.0	0
340	1.0	7,485.9	298.9	96.0	0
408	1.2	7,485.9	265.8	97.0	0
476	1.4	7,485.9	265.8	97.0	0
544	1.6	7,485.9	265.8	97.0	0
612	1.8	7,485.9	265.8	97.0	0
680	2.0	7,485.9	234.5	97.0	0
1,020	3.0	7,485.9	186.0	98.0	0
1,360	4.0	7,485.9	186.0	98.0	0
2,040	6.0	7,485.9	186.0	98.0	0
2,720	8.0	7,485.9	186.0	98.0	0

This report listing clearly shows that there is enough *pga_aggregate_target* set as there are no single or multi-pass sort executions. From the data file I/O section of the report, one can also see that there was no I/O to the temporary tablespace, again indicating all sort and hash type activity was accomplished in memory.

If there was a maximum value for *pga_aggregate_target* or the DBA wanted to reduce the setting to allow more users to utilize the system, the temporary tablespace could be moved to SSD and deliberately force sorts and hash operations to the temporary tablespace.

The next section of the AWRRPT report deals with the SHARED pool, JAVA pool and buffer statistics. This report section is shown in the following listing:

```
Shared Pool Advisory  DB/Inst: SSD/ssd2  Snap: 4
-> SP: Shared Pool      Est LC: Estimated Library Cache    Factr: Factor
-> Note there is often a 1:Many correlation between a single logical object
   in the Library Cache, and the physical number of memory objects associated
   with it.   Therefore comparing the number of Lib Cache objects (e.g. in
   v$librarycache), with the number of Lib Cache Memory Objects is invalid.


                                    Est LC Est LC  Est LC Est LC
      Shared    SP   Est LC           Time   Time    Load   Load          Est LC
        Pool  Size     Size   Est LC  Saved  Saved   Time   Time             Mem
     Size(M) Factr      (M)  Mem Obj    (s)  Factr    (s)  Factr        Obj Hits
     ------- -----  ------- -------- ------ ------ ------- ------  -----------
          76    .3       13    1,954     12    1.0       6    1.0        15,331
         104    .4       13    1,954     12    1.0       6    1.0        15,331
         132    .5       13    1,954     12    1.0       6    1.0        15,331
         160    .7       13    1,954     12    1.0       6    1.0        15,331
         188    .8       13    1,954     12    1.0       6    1.0        15,331
         216    .9       13    1,954     12    1.0       6    1.0        15,331
         244   1.0       13    1,954     12    1.0       6    1.0        15,331
         272   1.1       13    1,954     12    1.0       6    1.0        15,331
         300   1.2       13    1,954     12    1.0       6    1.0        15,331
         328   1.3       13    1,954     12    1.0       6    1.0        15,331
         356   1.5       13    1,954     12    1.0       6    1.0        15,331
         384   1.6       13    1,954     12    1.0       6    1.0        15,331
         412   1.7       13    1,954     12    1.0       6    1.0        15,331
         440   1.8       13    1,954     12    1.0       6    1.0        15,331
         468   1.9       13    1,954     12    1.0       6    1.0        15,331
         496   2.0       13    1,954     12    1.0       6    1.0        15,331
            --------------------------------------------------------------

Java Pool Advisory  DB/Inst: SSD/ssd2  Snap: 4

                No data exists for this section of the report.
            --------------------------------------------------------------

Buffer Wait Statistics  DB/Inst: SSD/ssd2  Snaps: 3-4
-> ordered by wait time desc, waits desc

Class               Waits Total Wait Time (s)  Avg Time (ms)
------------------ ----------- -------------------- --------------
data block           1,304                   28               22
undo header            356                    2                4
undo block             195                    1                4
1st level bmb            4                    0                0
system undo header       1                    0                0
            --------------------------------------------------------------
```

In this section, it appears that the SHARED pool is possibly over allocated for this database. From a review of the advisory section

---

Using AWRRPT Reports

and the heading section back in the first report listing in this section, the memory assigned to the SHARED pool is not being fully used, and the JAVA pool is not being used at all.

The section of the above listing dealing with the Buffer Wait Statistics indicates a need to see why transactions are holding on to blocks as the *data block waits* are most likely due to transaction issues. The next section, the enqueue report, will shine some light on the possible causes of the *data block buffer waits*.

The enqueue section of the AWRRPT report is next. It shows statistics for the various enqueue resources that protect memory structures in the database and force serialization of access to shared resources. The following listing shows the report excerpt:

```
Enqueue Activity  DB/Inst: SSD/ssd2  Snaps: 3-4
-> Enqueue stats gathered prior to 10i should not be compared with 10i data
-> ordered by Wait Time desc, Waits desc

Enqueue Type (Request Reason)
-----------------------------------------------------------------------------
    Requests    Succ Gets Failed Gets      Waits  Wt Time (s) Av Wt Time(ms)
  ----------- ----------- ----------- ----------- ------------ --------------
TX-Transaction (row lock contention)
        202         202           0         200          213        1,065.90
TX-Transaction (allocate ITL entry)
          2           2           0           2            3        1,485.00
US-Undo Segment
        935         935           0          77            1           10.91
HW-Segment High Water Mark
        418         418           0         256            0             .39
CF-Controlfile Transaction
      5,365       5,365           0          83            0            1.20
FB-Format Block
         68          68           0          40            0             .75
TX-Transaction
      8,081       8,081           0          16            0            1.88
TX-Transaction (index contention)
         24          24           0          17            0            1.18
TS-Temporary Segment
         10          10           0           9            0            2.22
PS-PX Process Reservation
        102         102           0          24            0             .42
TT-Tablespace
        227         227           0          20            0             .00
TA-Instance Undo
         16          16           0          13            0             .00
WF-SWRF Flush
         11          11           0          11            0             .00
TM-DML
     33,886      33,886           0           6            0             .00
UL-User-defined
          6           6           0           6            0             .00
DR-Distributed Recovery
          2           2           0           2            0             .00
PI-Remote PX Process Spawn Status
```

```
              6              6              0              2              0            .00
AF-Advisor Framework (task serialization)
              7              7              0              1              0            .00
PW-Buffer Cache PreWarm (flush prewarm buffers)
              1              0              1              1              0            .00
IR-Instance Recovery
            114            114              0              1              0            .00
       --------------------------------------------------------------------------
```

Transaction based enqueues, TX and TL, dominate the report. These usually indicate transaction locking issues and block sharing issues in the application. It should be noted that this database was built using automatic segment space management tablespaces, and in some high transaction environments, these have shown ITL related waits, so that is probably what is seen here with the TL enqueues. The TX enqueues occur when an exclusive row lock is requested and it indicates processes are competing for the same data.

The AWRRPT report section deals with undo segments, the following shows this section of the report.

```
Undo Segment Summary  DB/Inst: SSD/ssd2  Snaps: 3-4
-> Undo segment block stats:
-> uS - unexpired Stolen,   uR - unexpired Released,   uU - unexpired reUsed
-> eS - expired  Stolen,    eR - expired  Released,    eU - expired   reUsed

Undo          Undo          Num  Max Qry  Max Tx   Snap  OutOf    uS/uR/uU/
TS#          Blocks        Trans Len (s) Concurcy TooOld Space    eS/eR/eU
----  ------------  --------------- -------- -------- ------ ----- --------------
  -
    5         2,770           8,792       38       44      0     0 0/0/0/0/0/0
       -------------------------------------------------------------------------

Undo Segment Stats  DB/Inst: SSD/ssd2  Snaps: 3-4
-> ordered by Time desc

                  Undo          Num Max Qry  Max Tx  Snap OutOf    uS/uR/uU/
End Time         Blocks        Trans Len (s) Concy TooOld Space    eS/eR/eU
-----------  ------------ ------------ ------- -------- ------ ----- -----------
  -
28-Jul 20:02          123          141       0       3      0     0 0/0/0/0/0/0
28-Jul 19:52            5           36       0       1      0     0 0/0/0/0/0/0
28-Jul 19:42          423        1,433       0      38      0     0 0/0/0/0/0/0
28-Jul 19:32          747        2,631      22      39      0     0 0/0/0/0/0/0
28-Jul 19:22          687        2,211      38      44      0     0 0/0/0/0/0/0
28-Jul 19:12          365        1,276       0      34      0     0 0/0/0/0/0/0
28-Jul 19:02          420        1,064       0      16      0     0 0/0/0/0/0/0
       -------------------------------------------------------------------------
```

From this report, the stress on the undo segments can be determined. In the example above, there were no *snapshot too old* errors and no undo segment ran *out of space*. In an OLTP type benchmark, an experienced DBA would not expect to see *out of space* or *snapshot too old* errors. The high number of transactions per undo segments should be noted as this could be why some undo contention exists. However, since the database was using automated undo management, there is not much benefit to using SSD.

The next few sections of the report deal with latches. The first two will be skipped as their use in tuning has been found to be minimal. The third one which deals with latch sleeps and spins is of interest. The listing below shows an example Latch Sleeps report from the AWRRPT report.

```
Latch Sleep Breakdown  DB/Inst: SSD/ssd2  Snaps: 3-4
-> ordered by misses desc

Latch Name
------------------------------------------
   Get Requests     Misses      Sleeps  Spin Gets   Sleep1   Sleep2   Sleep3
-------------- ----------- ----------- ---------- -------- -------- --------
cache buffers chains
    12,875,058       1,550       1,045        990      110      425       25
library cache lock
        26,765         444          96        352       88        4        0
cache buffers lru chain
       230,511         200          20        180       20        0        0
library cache
       231,516         183          29        154       29        0        0
row cache objects
       101,189         160           2        158        2        0        0
enqueue hash chains
       241,402         148           2        146        2        0        0
session allocation
        38,907         102          58         53       41        7        1
KCL gc element parent latch
       587,433          89          26         70       12        7        0
gcs resource hash
       486,587          80           1         79        1        0        0
ges enqueue table freelist
        78,029          62           2         60        2        0        0
library cache pin
       173,817          53           7         46        7        0        0
ges resource hash list
        88,560          53           6         47        6        0        0
messages
       208,554          30           2         28        2        0        0
undo global data
        76,852          26           1         25        1        0        0
enqueues
        95,817          18           1         17        1        0        0
shared pool
       106,889          17           2         15        2        0        0
redo allocation
        32,950          12           2         10        2        0        0
KJC message pool free list
        15,059           5           1          4        1        0        0
slave class create
             8           1           1          0        1        0        0
          -------------------------------------------------------------
```

When a process requests a latch and there is no latch available, the process spins and waits for the latch. This is known as a latch sleep, and high numbers of sleeps for a particular latch indicate that some tuning effort may be required in the area of the Oracle system in which the latch is located. In the example report, the highest sleeps are in the area of the buffer cache and library caches. These could be due to transaction issues. They could also be due to a particular area being too large, which is not evident in this case. In all actuality for the activity level in this database, the values are probably acceptable and would be corrected by correcting the transaction problems previously noted.

The next section of the report breaks the latches into their child components. While this is interesting from a tuning perspective, it really is not in the purview of this book, so the segment I/O statistics sections will be covered next. The first section deals with segment physical and logical reads. Examples of these sections are shown in the following listing:

```
Segments by Logical Reads  DB/Inst: SSD/ssd2  Snaps: 3-4
-> % Total shows % of logical reads for each top segment compared with total
   logical reads for all segments captured by the Snapshot

           Tablespace                      Subobject  Obj.      Logical
Owner      Name        Object Name         Name       Type       Reads
%Total
---------- ----------  ------------------- ---------- -----  ------------ ------
TPCC       USERS       C_ORDER                        TABLE   5,125,520  85.29
TPCC       USERS       C_STOCK_I1                     INDEX     358,688   5.97
TPCC       USERS       C_STOCK                        TABLE     128,976   2.15
TPCC       USERS       C_ITEM_I1                      INDEX      74,128   1.23
TPCC       USERS       C_ORDER_LINE_I1                INDEX      58,064    .97
                       ------------------------------------------------------

Segments by Physical Reads  DB/Inst: SSD/ssd2  Snaps: 3-4

           Tablespace                      Subobject  Obj.     Physical
Owner      Name        Object Name         Name       Type      Reads %Total
---------- ----------  ------------------- ---------- -----  ------------ ------
TPCC       USERS       C_CUSTOMER                     TABLE       3,050  55.53
TPCC       USERS       C_ORDER_LINE                   TABLE         847  15.42
TPCC       USERS       C_ORDER_LINE_I1                INDEX         666  12.12
TPCC       USERS       C_STOCK                        TABLE         533   9.70
TPCC       USERS       C_CUSTOMER_I2                  INDEX         208   3.79
                       ------------------------------------------------------
```

The above listing indicates that the majority of I/O was logical in nature. This is to be expected, of course, since the system is nearly 100% cached in the database data buffers. There is some physical I/O for cache replacement activities and other database upkeep activity such as commits, rollbacks, and DML related events. In an environment where one considers using SSD, this report would be used to isolate specific objects that would benefit from being placed on possibly limited SSD resources, choosing to move high I/O objects from the normal disk array to the SSD.

The second third of the segment I/O report shows segments that have undergone various wait activities. This report section is handy for isolating objects which might need tuning or are involved in transactions (SQL) that might need tuning. The following listing is an example of this part of the AWRRPT:

```
Segments by Buffer Busy Waits  DB/Inst: SSD/ssd2  Snaps: 3-4
                                                         Buffer
              Tablespace                    Subobject  Obj.   Busy
Owner         Name       Object Name        Name       Type   Waits %Total
----------    ----------  ------------------ ---------- -----  ------------ ------
TPCC          USERS       C_DISTRICT                    TABLE     70  72.16
TPCC          USERS       C_WAREHOUSE                   TABLE     14  14.43
TPCC          USERS       C_ORDER_LINE                  TABLE      5   5.15
TPCC          USERS       C_ORDER_LINE_I1               INDEX      3   3.09
SYS           SYSTEM      SEG$                          TABLE      2   2.06
              ------------------------------------------------------------

Segments by Row Lock Waits  DB/Inst: SSD/ssd2  Snaps: 3-4
                                                         Row
              Tablespace                    Subobject  Obj.   Lock
Owner         Name       Object Name        Name       Type   Waits %Total
----------    ----------  ------------------ ---------- -----  ------------ ------
TPCC          USERS       C_DISTRICT                    TABLE    354  82.71
TPCC          USERS       C_STOCK                       TABLE     32   7.48
TPCC          USERS       C_NEW_ORDER                   TABLE     16   3.74
TPCC          USERS       C_ORDER_LINE_I1               INDEX     12   2.80
TPCC          USERS       C_ORDER_I1                    INDEX      9   2.10
              ------------------------------------------------------------

Segments by ITL Waits  DB/Inst: SSD/ssd2  Snaps: 3-4
              No data exists for this section of the report.
              ------------------------------------------------------------
```

The above listing shows that the same objects are showing *buffer busy waits* as are showing *row lock waits*. Again, this points to transaction locking as the cause for the *buffer busy waits* and ties back also to the large number of TX enqueues noted in previous report section listings.

The last third of the Segment report section deals with RAC I/O and is particularly interesting as it shows the objects most transferred across the interconnect. The following listing shows the RAC Segment I/O report for the global cache service based transfers of blocks:

```
Segments by CR Blocks Received  DB/Inst: SSD/ssd2  Snaps: 3-4

                                                          CR
               Tablespace                    Subobject Obj.  Blocks
Owner          Name       Object Name        Name      Type  Received %Total
----------     ---------- ------------------ --------- ----- --------- ------
TPCC           USERS      C_STOCK                      TABLE    20,761  41.50
TPCC           USERS      C_ORDER                      TABLE    11,166  22.32
TPCC           USERS      C_ORDER_LINE_I1              INDEX     4,746   9.49
TPCC           USERS      C_DISTRICT                   TABLE     3,139   6.27
TPCC           USERS      C_WAREHOUSE                  TABLE     2,813   5.62
               ------------------------------------------------------------

Segments by Current Blocks Received  DB/Inst: SSD/ssd2  Snaps: 3-4

                                                        Current
               Tablespace                    Subobject Obj.  Blocks
Owner          Name       Object Name        Name      Type  Received %Total
----------     ---------- ------------------ --------- ----- --------- ------
TPCC           USERS      C_STOCK                      TABLE    16,523  44.48
TPCC           USERS      C_DISTRICT                   TABLE     3,079   8.29
TPCC           USERS      C_NEW_ORDER_I1               INDEX     3,041   8.19
TPCC           USERS      C_ORDER                      TABLE     2,977   8.01
TPCC           USERS      C_ORDER_LINE_I1              INDEX     2,884   7.76
               ------------------------------------------------------------
```

This listing makes it easy to see what segments have blocks being transferred across the interconnect. In a move to SSD in a RAC environment, these segments should be considered as possible targets to be placed on SSD.

The next AWRRPT report section deals with dictionary and library cache statistics. An item to watch for in a RAC environment is excessive sequence activity as this can indicate that the sequences are not properly configured for a RAC environment. For example, to be RAC Safe, a sequence should be cached, *nocycle* and *noorder*. The following listing shows the dictionary and library reports:

```
Dictionary Cache Stats  DB/Inst: SSD/ssd2  Snaps: 3-4
-> "Pct Misses"  should be very low (< 2% in most cases)
-> "Final Usage" is the number of cache entries being used

                             Get     Pct    Scan    Pct     Mod      Final
Cache                    Requests    Miss    Reqs    Miss    Reqs     Usage
--------------------     --------    ----    ----    ----    --------  ------
dc_awr_control                 62    3.2       0                0          1
dc_global_oids             1,137    0.0       0                0         22
dc_histogram_defs            110    0.0       0                0      2,285
dc_object_ids              1,507    0.3       0                0        558
dc_objects                   436    5.0       0                0        621
dc_profiles                   85    0.0       0                0          1
dc_rollback_segments      17,403    0.1       0               30         98
dc_segments                  175    8.6       0               41        369
dc_sequences                  14   35.7       0               14          6
dc_tablespace_quotas           2    0.0       0                2          1
dc_tablespaces             5,004    0.0       0                0          7
dc_usernames                 298    0.0       0                0         11
dc_users                   8,822    0.0       0                0         38
outstanding_alerts            36   66.7       0                0          5
                      ----------------------------------------------------

Dictionary Cache Stats (RAC)  DB/Inst: SSD/ssd2  Snaps: 3-4

                             GES         GES         GES
Cache                    Requests   Conflicts    Releases
--------------------     --------   ---------    --------
dc_awr_control                  2           2           0
dc_object_ids                   5           0           0
dc_objects                     22           0           0
dc_rollback_segments           57           1           0
dc_segments                    84           4           0
dc_sequences                   24           4           0
dc_tablespace_quotas            4           0           0
outstanding_alerts             72          24           0
                      ----------------------------------------------------

Library Cache Activity  DB/Inst: SSD/ssd2  Snaps: 3-4
-> "Pct Misses"  should be very low

                     Get     Pct           Pin    Pct              Invali-
Namespace        Requests    Miss      Requests    Miss    Reloads  dations
---------------  --------    ----    ---------    ----    -------  -------
BODY                   12    0.0            30    0.0          0        0
INDEX                   1    0.0             1    0.0          0        0
SQL AREA            3,111    0.1        77,182    0.0          2        0
TABLE/PROCEDURE        51    0.0         8,823    0.0          0        0
                      ----------------------------------------------------

Library Cache Activity (RAC)  DB/Inst: SSD/ssd2  Snaps: 3-4

                 GES Lock     GES Pin     GES Pin    GES Inval GES Invali-
Namespace        Requests    Requests    Releases    Requests    dations
---------------  --------    --------    --------    --------  -----------
INDEX                   1           0           0           0          0
TABLE/PROCEDURE       309           0           0           0          0
                      ----------------------------------------------------
```

There is a section for the above referenced section of the AWRRPT that is only present if the database is RAC enabled. This section shows the dictionary statistics for the dictionary cache for the global enqueue service as well as a library cache activity section for GES. As long as reloads and invalidations are kept to near zero, things are probably ok. The miss percent of

35% for *dc_sequences* probably indicates some of the instance sequences are not RAC safe.

The next AWRRPT report section deals with the breakdown of memory into the various SGA sections and pools. The first report in the following listing shows the various memory sections and their sizes. The next section in the listing shows how the memory profile may have changed during the period of time between the first snapshot and the second. This section of the report does not yield much helpful information on the use or non-use of SSD:

```
SGA Memory Summary  DB/Inst: SSD/ssd2  Snap: 4

SGA regions                     Size in Bytes
------------------------------  ----------------
Database Buffers                   805,306,368
Fixed Size                             782,544
Redo Buffers                           524,288
Variable Size                      267,128,624
SGA breakdown difference  DB/Inst: SSD/ssd2  Snaps: 3-4

Pool   Name                          Begin value         End value  % Diff
------ ----------------------  ----------------  ----------------  ------
java   free memory                    4,194,304         4,194,304    0.00
large  PX msg pool                      902,160           902,160    0.00
large  free memory                    3,292,144         3,292,144    0.00
shared ASH buffers                     4,194,304         4,194,304    0.00
shared KGLS heap                       2,463,820         2,463,820    0.00
shared KQR L SO                           45,056            45,056    0.00
shared KQR M PO                        1,779,792         1,793,616    0.78
shared KQR M SO                           50,688            50,688    0.00
shared KQR S PO                          124,224           130,624    5.15
shared KQR S SO                            4,096             4,096    0.00
shared KSXR receive buffers            1,032,500         1,032,500    0.00
shared PL/SQL DIANA                    1,424,592         1,424,592    0.00
shared PL/SQL MPCODE                   1,371,980         1,371,980    0.00
shared PLS non-lib hp                     11,168            11,168    0.00
shared PX subheap                        131,068           131,068    0.00
shared dbwriter coalesce buffer        1,049,088         1,049,088    0.00
shared event statistics per sess       3,860,360         3,860,360    0.00
shared fixed allocation callback             428               428    0.00
shared free memory                   158,959,480       158,216,716   -0.47
shared gcs resources                  16,900,480        16,900,480    0.00
shared gcs shadows                     6,893,064         6,893,064    0.00
shared ges big msg buffers             3,013,444         3,013,444    0.00
shared ges enqueues                    2,224,400         2,247,808    1.05
shared ges reserved msg buffers        1,238,404         1,238,404    0.00
shared ges resources                   1,475,496         1,492,872    1.18
shared joxs heap                           4,220             4,220    0.00
shared library cache                   8,487,496         8,874,140    4.56
shared miscellaneous                  25,591,776        25,647,460    0.22
shared parameters                         51,908            51,908    0.00
shared partitioning d                    133,692           133,692    0.00
shared pl/sql source                      17,732            17,732    0.00
shared repository                         57,636            57,636    0.00
shared row cache                       3,707,272         3,707,272    0.00
shared sql area                        9,220,432         9,459,860    2.60
shared table definiti                        952               952    0.00
shared trigger defini                      3,248             3,248    0.00
```

```
shared trigger inform                    1,944              1,944    0.00
shared trigger source                    7,616              7,616    0.00
shared type object de                  318,688            318,688    0.00
      buffer_cache                   805,306,368        805,306,368    0.00
      fixed_sga                        782,544            782,544    0.00
      log_buffer                       524,288            524,288    0.00
      --------------------------------------------------------------
```

The Resource Activity report is next. This is another new section for the Oracle10g AWRRPT over the old STATSPACK type reports. The following listing shows an example of the Resource report:

```
Resource Limit Stats  DB/Inst: SSD/ssd2  Snap: 4
-> only rows with Current or Maximum Utilization > 80% of Limit are shown
-> ordered by resource name

                         Current      Maximum    Initial
Resource Name          Utilization  Utilization Allocation   Limit
-------------------    ------------ ------------ ----------  --------
gcs_resources                   640      106,592     106592    106592
gcs_shadows                  36,610       91,052     106592    106592
ges_procs                        24          149        151       151
processes                        24          150        150       150
sessions                         28          154        170       170
      --------------------------------------------------------------
```

In the report section in the above listing, the various systems related GCS and GES limits are available. If it appears that the environment is approaching one of the limits, the DBA may need to perform analysis and tuning to correct it.

The next section of the report simply shows the initialization parameters that are different from the default settings. This is not really important except with regard to tuning activities, so it will be skipped. After the initialization parameter section, the AWRRPT report adds a global enqueue statistics section. This section appears earlier in the report lineup in a STATSPACK report. The following shows a partial listing of this report section:

```
Global Enqueue Statistics  DB/Inst: SSD/ssd2  Snaps: 3-4

Statistic                              Total    per Second   per Trans
----------------------------------  ----------- ------------ ------------
gcs assume no cvt                        21,317         5.9          2.8
gcs blocked converts                     38,736        10.7          5.1
gcs blocked cr converts                  60,525        16.7          8.0
gcs compatible basts                          1         0.0          0.0
gcs compatible cr basts (global)          2,481         0.7          0.3
gcs compatible cr basts (local)           1,551         0.4          0.2
gcs dbwr flush pi msgs                    8,784         2.4          1.2
```

```
gcs dbwr write request msgs             6,942      1.9       0.9
gcs immediate (compatible) conver       2,008      0.6       0.3
gcs immediate (null) converts           3,258      0.9       0.4
gcs immediate cr (compatible) con       1,679      0.5       0.2
gcs immediate cr (null) converts        1,784      0.5       0.2
gcs indirect ast                        5,446      1.5       0.7
gcs lms write request msgs              1,167      0.3       0.2
gcs msgs process time(ms)               8,482      2.3       1.1
gcs msgs received                     158,053     43.5      20.9
gcs retry convert request               5,429      1.5       0.7
gcs side channel msgs actual              562      0.2       0.1
gcs side channel msgs logical          98,668     27.2      13.1
gcs write notification msgs               926      0.3       0.1
gcs writes refused                         16      0.0       0.0
ges msgs process time(ms)                  63      0.0       0.0
ges msgs received                       6,023      1.7       0.8
implicit batch messages received        1,783      0.5       0.2
implicit batch messages sent            3,426      0.9       0.5
messages flow controlled                1,055      0.3       0.1
messages queue sent actual             28,608      7.9       3.8
messages queue sent logical            37,033     10.2       4.9
messages received actual              137,220     37.8      18.2
messages received logical             164,076     45.2      21.7
messages sent directly                 99,375     27.4      13.2
messages sent indirectly               36,838     10.1       4.9
messages sent not implicit batche      25,182      6.9       3.3
messages sent pbatched                 43,929     12.1       5.8
msgs causing lmd to send msgs           3,009      0.8       0.4
msgs causing lms(s) to send msgs       13,414      3.7       1.8
msgs received queue time (ms)             883      0.2       0.1
msgs received queued                  164,076     45.2      21.7
msgs sent queue time (ms)               1,011      0.3       0.1
msgs sent queue time on ksxp (ms)      76,689     21.1      10.2
msgs sent queued                       36,744     10.1       4.9
msgs sent queued on ksxp              131,507     36.2      17.4
process batch messages received        30,869      8.5       4.1
process batch messages sent            33,877      9.3       4.5
          --------------------------------------------------------
```

The report section in the above is more useful for monitoring
and tuning the RAC interconnect environment; however, its
values can help determine if the interconnect is being stressed.
The stress on the interconnect will show itself as high values for
the various time parameters shown in the Global Enqueue
Statistics report section of the AWRRPT report.

The final section of the report deals with the Global Cache
Statistics (GCS). The following sample listing shows the GCS
Statistics section of the AWRRPT Report:

```
Global CR Served Stats  DB/Inst: SSD/ssd2  Snaps: 3-4
Statistic                              Total
------------------------------    ------------------
CR Block Requests                      64,210
CURRENT Block Requests                  5,353
Data Block Requests                    64,210
Undo Block Requests                     1,231
TX Block Requests                       4,122
Current Results                        67,165
```

```
Private results                           593
Zero Results                            1,806
Disk Read Results                           0
Fail Results                                0
Fairness Down Converts                  8,529
Fairness Clears                             0
Free GC Elements                            0
Flushes                                 2,907
Flushes Queued                              0
Flush Queue Full                            0
Flush Max Time (us)                   139,047
Light Works                               998
Errors                                      0
        ---------------------------------------
Global CURRENT Served Stats  DB/Inst: SSD/ssd2  Snaps: 3-4
-> Pins    = CURRENT Block Pin Operations
-> Flushes = Redo Flush before CURRENT Block Served Operations
-> Writes  = CURRENT Block Fusion Write Operations

Statistic      Total   % <1ms  % <10ms % <100ms   % <1s   % <10s
---------- ------------- -------- -------- -------- -------- --------
Pins          41,766    99.57     0.02     0.41    0.00     0.00
Flushes          216     4.63    27.78    67.59    0.00     0.00
Writes         9,462    72.29    12.63    15.07    0.01     0.00
        --------------------------------------------------------------
```

In the GCS statistics report, the stress on the interconnect can be tracked by reviewing the timing histograms provided for pins, flushes, and writes. If the times shown skew to the right side of the histogram, as indicated in the listing with the flushes timings, the interconnect is showing some stress.

The following section will conclude the technical information in this chapter by reviewing the STATSPACK runs from the TPC-H SSD runs.

Example STATSPACK Results from the TPC-H SSD Runs

This section will provide a review of the STATSPACK report for the same query and data profiles against the SSD array instead of the SCSI/ATA arrays. The following listing shows the top five wait events from SSD run number five:

```
Instance Efficiency Percentages (Target 100%)
~~~~~~~~~~~~~~~~~~~~~~~~~~~~~~~~~~~~~~~~~~~~~~~~
            Buffer Nowait %:  100.00      Redo NoWait %:  100.00
             Buffer  Hit  %:   18.83   In-memory Sort %:   99.67
             Library Hit  %:   98.72       Soft Parse %:   98.55
          Execute to Parse %:   67.94       Latch Hit %:  100.00
Parse CPU to Parse Elapsd %:  150.00   % Non-Parse CPU:  100.00

   Shared Pool Statistics        Begin    End
                                 ------   ------
                Memory Usage %:   47.18   48.16
     % SQL with executions>1:    79.52   84.83
     % Memory for SQL w/exec>1:  64.58   80.39

Top 5 Timed Events
~~~~~~~~~~~~~~~~~~~                                                  % Total
Event                                      Waits    Time (s) Ela Time
----------------------------------------- ------------ ----------- --------
CPU time                                                     2,962    72.43
db file scattered read                    1,630,994    1,101    26.92
db file parallel read                         6,373       16      .39
db file sequential read                      80,346        7      .18
control file parallel write                   1,831        3      .07
                          ------------------------------------------------
```

The waits are still occurring for the I/O just as they were for the
SCSI and ATA runs; however, they are now less than the CPU
related waits. The I/O profile from the run five report shows the
majority of I/O going against the data and index datafiles similar
to the SCSI and ATA array results. The following listing shows
the I/O profile for the SSD array from the same STATSPACK
report as the listing immediately above:

```
File I/O Stats for DB: DSS  Instance: dss  Snaps: 1 -2
->ordered by Tablespace, File
Tablespace                    Filename
----------------------        --------------------------------------------
                  Av     Av    Av                       Av      Buffer Av Buf
          Reads Reads/s Rd(ms) Blks/Rd      Writes Writes/s    Waits Wt(ms)
--------------  ------- ------ -------  ------------ --------  ------ ------
DSS_DATA                      /u01/oracle/oradata/dss/dss_data01.dbf
        648,400     115   0.6   11.4         0         0          0
                             /u02/oracle/oradata/dss/dss_data02.dbf
        571,656     102   0.6   11.5         0         0          0
                             /u03/oracle/oradata/dss/dss_data03.dbf
        581,510     103   0.6   11.5         0         0          0
DSS_INDEX                    /u04/oracle/oradata/dss/dss_index01.dbf
          4,029       1   0.2    2.7         0         0          0
                             /u06/oracle/oradata/dss/dss_index02.dbf
          3,815       1   0.2    2.8         0         0          0
                             /u07/oracle/oradata/dss/dss_index03.dbf
          3,944       1   0.2    2.8         0         0          0
PERFSTAT                     /u05/oracle/oradata/dss/perfstat01.dbf
              3       0   0.0   10.0       803         0          0
SYSTEM                       /u01/oracle/oradata/dss/system01.dbf
             50       0   0.4    3.2       350         0          0
TEMP                         /u05/oracle/oradata/dss/temp1.dbf
         19,568       3   1.3   13.2    20,621         4          0
UNDOTBS1                     /u02/oracle/oradata/dss/undotbs101.dbf
              0       0                    60         0          0
                             /u04/oracle/oradata/dss/undotbs102.dbf
              0       0                    32         0          0
                             /u05/oracle/oradata/dss/undotbs103.dbf
              4       0   0.0    1.0       132         0          0
                          ------------------------------------------------
```

From a review of the STATSPACK report from SSD run six with reduced buffer cache, there is not much evidence of a shift in the profile based on the loss of 500 megabytes of preloaded data. This is shown in the following listing. In fact, the hit ratio increased:

```
Instance Efficiency Percentages (Target 100%)
~~~~~~~~~~~~~~~~~~~~~~~~~~~~~~~~~~~~~~~~~~~~~~~
            Buffer Nowait %:  100.00      Redo NoWait %:  100.00
            Buffer  Hit   %:   20.31   In-memory Sort %:   99.66
            Library Hit   %:   93.73        Soft Parse %:   94.71
          Execute to Parse %:   58.87        Latch Hit %:  100.00
Parse CPU to Parse Elapsd %:    4.53     % Non-Parse CPU:   99.98

   Shared Pool Statistics        Begin    End
                                 ------   ------
                Memory Usage %:  33.65    37.94
       % SQL with executions>1:  52.23    60.09
      % Memory for SQL w/exec>1: 35.76    54.60

Top 5 Timed Events
~~~~~~~~~~~~~~~~~~                                                % Total
Event                                   Waits    Time (s) Ela Time
-------------------------------------- ------------ ----------- --------
CPU time                                            2,473     69.78
db file scattered read                 1,313,555    1,026     28.95
db file parallel read                      6,564       26       .72
control file parallel write                1,194       10       .29
db file sequential read                   36,043        6       .17
                                       -------------------------------------
```

While the shift is there, it is only a couple of percentage points. Compare the time, in seconds, waiting for the read events in the above listing with the ATA array results listing shown in the previous section in this chapter titled "Reviewing the STATSPACK Report for SSD." The total wait events and their associated wait times where reduced by a factor of 376 when compared to those in the ATA array results based on total wait time for I/O related events.

The following section will cover more systems that might benefit from a move to SSD base on analysis of waits and file I/O characteristics.

When a System Will Not Benefit From Moving to SSD

The move to SSD assets from standard SCSI, ATA or SATA disks can be a blessing when it answers a specific performance problem related to disk I/O saturation. However, one must be careful when diagnosing the I/O related problems on a system. This section will provide some example STATSPACKs and use them to show whether or not there is a benefit to moving to SSD assets.

The following listing includes an events report for a system that will not benefit from SSD:

```
Top 5 Timed Events
~~~~~~~~~~~~~~~~~~~                                          % Total
Event                                     Waits  Time (s) Ela Time
--------------------------------------- -------- --------- --------
CPU time                                            1,127    73.25
global cache cr request                  213,187      122     7.95
db file sequential read                  152,521       96     6.27
control file sequential read             118,104       78     5.06
SQL*Net message from dblink                  890       38     2.48
                                                 ---------
```

The system in the above listing spends 73% of its time in the CPU with only 11 percent of the time spent waiting on disks. If the system were tuned to eliminate the CPU bottleneck, chances are the bottleneck will move to the disks and at that time, it would benefit from SSD technology. As the system in the listing stands right now, moving to SSD could actually hurt performance as it would place more stress on the already over worked CPU assets.

In the next example, the move to SSD might be beneficial since there is reserve CPU capacity of 40%, and it is spending the other wait time waiting on disks as shown in the following listing:

```
Top 5 Timed Events
~~~~~~~~~~~~~~~~~~~                                          % Total
Event                                     Waits  Time (s) Ela Time
--------------------------------------- -------- --------- --------
CPU time                                            1,300    60.46
db file sequential read                  342,625      616    28.67
```

```
db file scattered read                              12,986      66    3.07
log file parallel write                              2,889      65    3.03
db file parallel write                               1,080      59    2.75
---------------------------------------------------------------------
```

The system in the above listing indicates index and table stress as well as stress on log files. Assuming that the sample amount of time in the STATSPACK is representative of the overall system performance, the DBA needs to look further to determine what should be moved, tables or indexes, to the SSD asset. The file I/O profile from this same report is shown in the following listing:

```
Tablespace
------------------------------
              Av      Av    Av                   Av         Buffer Av Buf
        Reads Reads/s Rd(ms) Blks/Rd  Writes Writes/s      Waits  Wt(ms)
------------ ------- ------ -------  ------------ --------  ---------- ------
SRCD
        12,680     4    6.7    1.0    18,943      6            0    0.0
SYSTEM
        30,282    10    3.0    2.5       623      0            0    0.0
UNDOTBS1
            14     0   35.7    1.0    28,733      9            0    0.0
SRCX
         2,799     1    4.5    1.0    18,038      6            0    0.0
NOMADD
        16,604     5    1.8    1.0         8      0            0    0.0
TST_GLOBALX
         7,560     2    1.6    1.0        18      0            0    0.0
TST_GLOBALD
         6,242     2    2.0    1.2        36      0            0    0.0
XDB
         5,636     2    1.5    1.0         4      0            0    0.0
REEX
         4,240     1    2.0    1.0         4      0            0    0.0
ZENX
         3,812     1    2.1    1.0         4      0            0    0.0
ESRX
         3,656     1    1.6    1.0         4      0            0    0.0
```

The heavy-hitters in this listing are the *srcd*, *system*, *nomad*, *tst_globallx* and *tst_globald* tablespaces. The actual report from which the listing is extracted is over ten pages long for this section on datafiles, but these are the largest contributors to the I/O profile. Analysis of the system showed improper use of the SYSTEM tablespace. Once this was corrected, the others were left as the I/O stress points. Moving the heavy hitters to an SSD asset would do the following for this system:

- Shift the load to the CPUs

- Reduce I/O stress on the I/O subsystem allowing other datafiles to be accessed more efficiently.

- Speed access to the data/indexes contained in the moved datafiles.

The above benefits might actually provide greater than the percentage benefit quoted above. One of the other waits deals with redo log files, specifically *log file parallel write*. Since this is a log file write specific wait, moving the redo logs would also show some benefit but not as great as that shown by moving tables and indexes.

The following listing provides a false positive indicator for use of SSD:

```
Top 5 Timed Events
~~~~~~~~~~~~~~~~~~                                            % Total
Event                               Waits    Time (s) Ela Time
-----------------------------   ------------ ------------ --------
db file sequential read          6,261,550     691    96.72
control file parallel write          1,274      19     2.73
CPU time                                         2      .24
db file parallel write                  28       1      .14
db file scattered read               2,248       1      .12
                                ------------------------------------
```

What is a false positive indicator? In this case, the STATSPACK seems to indicate that the database is doing a lot of full table scans and that this is 96-97 percent of wait times, which should indicate a move to SSD would be beneficial. However, a review of the entire report should be conducted. The header for the file is shown in the following listing:

```
STATSPACK report for

DB Name        DB Id    Instance    Inst Num Release    Cluster Host
------------ ----------- ------------ -------- ----------- ------- ----------
TSTPRD       3265066449 tstprd             1 9.2.0.3.0   NO      test08

              Snap Id    Snap Time     Sessions Curs/Sess Comment
              ------- ------------------ -------- --------- --------------------
Begin Snap:         3 09-Nov-03 13:20:20      10     2.1
  End Snap:         4 09-Nov-03 14:26:01      10     2.1
  Elapsed:                65.68 (mins)

Cache Sizes (end)
~~~~~~~~~~~~~~~~~
              Buffer Cache:        24M   Std Block Size:        8K
          Shared Pool Size:        48M       Log Buffer:      512K
```

The tiny size for the buffer cache and shared pool should be noted along with the restricted time period monitored. Unless the server has severe memory limitations, the company using this database would be better off increasing the memory allocated to the instance and then looking at SSD if the waits are still an issue. The small elapsed time indicates that this STATSPACK run was probably for a specific transaction and is not indicative of full system load.

While a move to SSD may benefit many systems, the DBA should carefully review all information to ensure that another fix is not more appropriate.

Conclusion

This chapter has provided information about using STATSPACK and custom reports to determine if SSD assets would help a system. STATSPACK and AWRRPT reports, to be beneficial, must not target a specific transaction but should look at overall system load. DBA's need to be aware of the memory allocation profile for the database on which the STATSPACK was run. If the memory is a choke point and there are sufficient resources available, tuning should occur there first followed by an evaluation of SSD suitability. However, in a RAC environment, moving too much of the database into memory can result in slower overall response and less throughput.

In a standard non-RAC environment, SSD assets will only help if a system is experiencing I/O contention and then will only give back the performance lost from those I/O activities that it can replace memory I/Os for physical I/Os. In cases where system load is predominately I/O related, as in the benchmark study, significant performance gains can be realized.

In a RAC environment, pushing the I/O away from a slow interconnect can improve performance and overall throughput. Both the custom and Oracle provided reports may be used to determine the most beneficial objects to move to SSD in a RAC environment. Generally, these will be the ones experiencing either the most I/O or the most transfers across the interconnect.

So what does the future hold? With high performance storage technology, the focus of future development will have to be on optimizing the Oracle internal architecture. The next chapter will examine the possible architecture changes that SSD technology will force on the Oracle software system.

No-disk Oracle Architectures

A Look Into the Future

Anyone paying attention while reading this book should be coming to a conclusion that disks will soon be relegated to the job of acting as backing store to massive arrays of solid state drives. It is an inescapable result of the massive improvements in memory sizes and huge reductions in memory cost.

Even Oracle, with their moves towards CPU-based costing and away from I/O based costing models in the cost based optimizer, can see the writing on the wall: disks will soon be for backup only with the real power resting in solid state memory based data storage.

For years, Oracle and other database providers focused considerable time and money on squeezing the last drop of performance out of disk arrays. This consisted of tortuously minimizing I/O path length, reducing code branches, improving the bus architectures simply because the disks at the end of the chain just could not get much faster. Now, other users can reap the benefits of all that work by replacing the spinning rust with SSD.

What will this mean in the future? First, Oracle and other manufacturers will need to concentrate on the database internals to fully utilize the power and speed provided by SSD. Eventually, the entire I/O subsystem will be replaced by the memory subsystem. Gone will be the host bus adapters, fibre connects, and other disk related architectures as more efficient methods are developed for accessing this high speed, high capacity SSD resource. Future generations of users will ask if mechanical devices were ever really used to store data.

Current Architectures

So what is it that will be replaced? A typical modern Oracle server setup is shown in Figure 7.1.

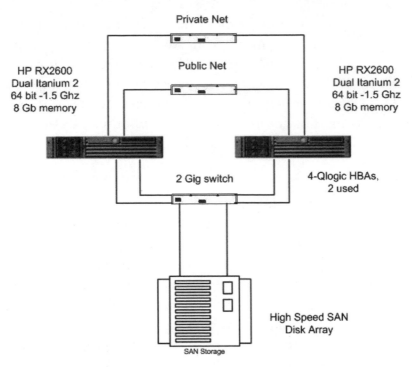

Figure 7.1: *Typical Modern Oracle RAC Configuration*

Figure 7.1 shows a typical RAC setup utilizing the most modern technologies: high speed interconnect; high speed HBA; and high speed network connections all leading to the Achilles heel in all architectures, the Storage Area Network (SAN or NAS) array with everything responding in microseconds except for the poor old spinning disks which are proud to do milliseconds. Even when RAM is stacked in front of the disks, the system will eventually reach the point where the cache is full and the system is once again forced back to the old disk limitations.

How would SSD look in the same configuration? For now, the SAN would be lopped off and the SSD put in its place as shown in Figure 7.2.

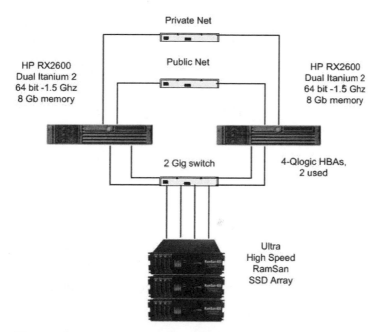

Figure 7.2: *Typical Modern Oracle RAC Configuration with RamSAN*

The move to RamSan is not arduous. In most environments, the switch is accomplished in a matter of hours, if not minutes. The time required to convert to SSD depends completely upon how fast the database and other files can be copied to the RamSan.

It is important to note that the number of channels accessing the RamSAN has been increased. With data bandwidth of up to 3000 MB/sec on the RamSAN400, the extra channels will be needed.

What Does this Mean to Oracle?

In the first round of testing using Oracle9i and the TPC-H benchmark, there was a test where the memory allocation to the database block buffers was reduced, and with the SSD drives, performance increased by several percent.

In an effort to gauge the importance of setting *db cache size* when using SSD assets, in run five of the TPC-H on SSD, the *db_cache_size* was reduced by 50% from one gigabyte to 500 megabytes. The results were surprising in that the overall run time was reduced by eight percent with most queries showing some improvement in runtime.

In the TPC-C study, tests were run with fully cached data. Subsequently, memory was reduced to 50% then to 25% of original settings. Overall, there was an increase in transactions per second and a decrease in average response and transaction times. In fact, with the increased memory available for users, the test was able to scale up to nearly 1000 direct connected users with no loss in response time or transaction times on only a 2-node, dual CPU setup.

This means that reading from disk is no longer a performance robber. With SSD, the disks are eliminated and they are replaced with high performance memory. Figure 7.3 shows the response time curve:

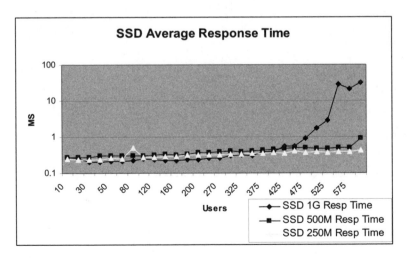

Figure 7.3: *SSD Response Time Curves for Various Memory Settings*

Figure 7.4 represents the same graph for the SATA setup:

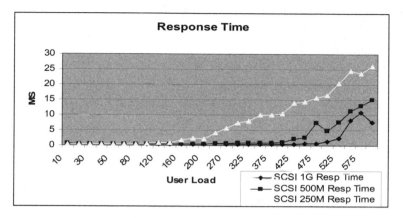

Figure 7.4: *SATA Response Time Curves for Various Memory Settings*

In this case, one picture, or chart in this case, is worth a thousand words.

What does this mean for the Oracle database of the future?

- The database cache will hold only a working size set of data

- No more huge disk farms

- No more disk failures, RAID arguments or struggling with backups

- The Program Global Area will take over as the main memory area, allowing unlimited sorts, hashes, sort-merge joins

- More users will be able to use the same equipment since more memory can be allocated to the process areas and less to the database

- Smaller, more efficient code bases for the Oracle database, reduced dependence on fancy LRU and aging algorithms.

Essentially, the relationship between the amount of data stored on SSD and the size of SGA caching areas is an inverse one. As the amount of data on SSDs goes up, the amount needed for database caching will decrease.

What about the other memory areas? As redo logs and undo segments go virtual, the redo log buffer will probably be phased out, eliminating it from the Oracle memory footprint. The undo segment will become the undo memory area. The roles of the various other pools, such as the SQL and JAVA pools, will still be used to ensure code is shared; however, whether they will still be utilized in the same fashion is not clear.

Once the database becomes virtualized into SSD, the entire internal structure of Oracle and the other databases will have to change. They will have to eliminate many of the structures, latches, locks that protected users from slow disks, delayed writes and many other evils associated with disks. The result should be a nearly quantum leap in processing speed.

Monitoring the Diskless Database

Before diskless Oracle, DBAs spent many restless nights.

Currently, DBAs spend an inordinate amount of time worrying about disk I/O, backups, and other topics that with the advent of a diskless Oracle environment will simply cease to exist. As more of the Oracle environment is virtualized, the monitoring has to change to more CPU cycle monitoring and effective use of CPU resources. This trend can already be identified with the larger footprint being taken by such topics as CPU costing. Soon, query cost will be counted not in terms of I/O to a disk but in CPU ticks and memory cycles.

What will be eliminated?

- Monitoring the cache: It will be automatically sized and tuned for the current working set only.

- Monitoring I/O speeds: Transfers will be at near memory speeds.

- Monitoring for contention: With no moving parts and hence greatly reduced latency, the SSD technology increases bandwidth by several orders of magnitude.

- Monitoring redo logs: They will simply be memory areas to be sized according to retention needs only.

- Monitoring undo segments: These will also become memory structures

- Monitoring backups: The SSD technology backs itself up. Offline backups of the backing store will not affect database performance.

The DBA's job as it is known today will undergo a profound change with more focus on tuning and optimization than worrying with physical hardware and backups.

But What About Now?

All of this information on improvements in the future is great, but what about now? What about the DBA that gets a RamSAN system? Does his job have to change? No. All monitoring that is done now can be done against the RamSAN system. The SSD is treated identically to a standard disk drive.

This means all of the DBA's scripts will still function as they always have. Monitoring tools will still act the same, but of course, they will report much better performance. Changing memory sizes should be done in a controlled fashion by reducing cache memory and testing performance until peak performance is reached. Preliminary testing shows the need to establish a working set size System Global Area (SGA) database cache which will vary from database to database.

Conclusion

Readers of this book should have, by now, reached the realization that things are about to undergo a profound change in the database universe. As RAM becomes cheaper and chips store more information, the cost of RAM SSD technology will also dramatically decline. A look at the overall management cost and hardware cost on a per transaction basis will reveal SSD technology to already be comparable to disk technology. In many ways, it will be superior.

It is time for progressive users to consider using SSD technology in those areas of their databases where it can deliver outstanding performance and bring their databases into the 21st century.

Index

TPC-C ERD and Tables

TPC-C ERD

The components of the TPC-C database are defined to consist of nine separate and individual tables. The relationships among these tables are defined in the entity relationship diagram shown below.

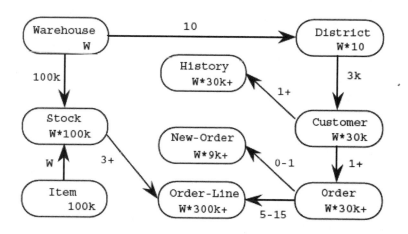

All numbers shown illustrate the database population requirements

- The numbers in the entity blocks represent the cardinality of the tables, the number of rows. These numbers are factored by W, the number of Warehouses, to illustrate the database scaling.

- The numbers next to the relationship arrows represent the cardinality of the relationships, the average number of children per parent.

- The plus (+) symbol is used after the cardinality of a relationship or table to illustrate that this number is subject to small variations in the initial database population over the measurement interval as rows are added or deleted.

TPC-C Table Structures

The tables utilized for the TPC-C benchmark must, at a minimum, have the following structures:

```
Description of C_CUSTOMER

Name                                       Null?    Type
----------------------------------------- -------- ------------------
 C_ID                                               NUMBER(5)
 C_D_ID                                             NUMBER(2)
 C_W_ID                                             NUMBER(4)
 C_FIRST                                            VARCHAR2(16)
 C_MIDDLE                                           CHAR(2)
 C_LAST                                             VARCHAR2(16)
 C_STREET_1                                         VARCHAR2(20)
 C_STREET_2                                         VARCHAR2(20)
 C_CITY                                             VARCHAR2(20)
 C_STATE                                            CHAR(2)
 C_ZIP                                              CHAR(9)
 C_PHONE                                            CHAR(16)
 C_SINCE                                            DATE
 C_CREDIT                                           CHAR(2)
 C_CREDIT_LIM                                       NUMBER(12,2)
 C_DISCOUNT                                         NUMBER(4,4)
 C_BALANCE                                          NUMBER(12,2)
 C_YTD_PAYMENT                                      NUMBER(12,2)
 C_PAYMENT_CNT                                      NUMBER(8)
 C_DELIVERY_CNT                                     NUMBER(8)
 C_DATA                                             VARCHAR2(500)

Description of C_DISTRICT

Name                                       Null?    Type
----------------------------------------- -------- ------------------
 D_ID                                               NUMBER(2)
 D_W_ID                                             NUMBER(4)
 D_YTD                                              NUMBER(12,2)
 D_TAX                                              NUMBER(4,4)
 D_NEXT_O_ID                                        NUMBER
 D_NAME                                             VARCHAR2(10)
 D_STREET_1                                         VARCHAR2(20)
 D_STREET_2                                         VARCHAR2(20)
 D_CITY                                             VARCHAR2(20)
```

```
    D_STATE                                          CHAR(2)
    D_ZIP                                            CHAR(9)

Description of C_HISTORY

Name                                     Null?    Type
---------------------------------------- -------- -----------------
    H_C_ID                                           NUMBER
    H_C_D_ID                                         NUMBER
    H_C_W_ID                                         NUMBER
    H_D_ID                                           NUMBER
    H_W_ID                                           NUMBER
    H_DATE                                           DATE
    H_AMOUNT                                         NUMBER(6,2)
    H_DATA                                           VARCHAR2(24)

Description of C_ITEM

Name                                     Null?    Type
---------------------------------------- -------- -----------------
    I_ID                                             NUMBER(6)
    I_IM_ID                                          NUMBER
    I_NAME                                           VARCHAR2(24)
    I_PRICE                                          NUMBER(5,2)
    I_DATA                                           VARCHAR2(50)

Description of C_NEW_ORDER

Name                                     Null?    Type
---------------------------------------- -------- -----------------
    NO_O_ID                                          NUMBER
    NO_D_ID                                          NUMBER
    NO_W_ID                                          NUMBER

Description of C_ORDER

Name                                     Null?    Type
---------------------------------------- -------- -----------------
    O_ID                                             NUMBER
    O_D_ID                                           NUMBER
    O_W_ID                                           NUMBER
    O_C_ID                                           NUMBER
    O_ENTRY_D                                        DATE
    O_CARRIER_ID                                     NUMBER
    O_OL_CNT                                         NUMBER
    O_ALL_LOCAL                                      NUMBER

Description of C_ORDER_LINE

Name                                     Null?    Type
---------------------------------------- -------- -----------------
    OL_O_ID                                          NUMBER
    OL_D_ID                                          NUMBER
    OL_W_ID                                          NUMBER
    OL_NUMBER                                        NUMBER
    OL_DELIVERY_D                                    DATE
    OL_I_ID                                          NUMBER
    OL_SUPPLY_W_ID                                   NUMBER
    OL_QUANTITY                                      NUMBER
    OL_AMOUNT                                        NUMBER(6,2)
    OL_DIST_INFO                                     CHAR(24)

Description of C_STOCK
```

```
Name                                      Null?     Type
---------------------------------------- --------- ------------------
 S_I_ID                                             NUMBER(6)
 S_W_ID                                             NUMBER(4)
 S_QUANTITY                                         NUMBER(6)
 S_DIST_01                                          CHAR(24)
 S_DIST_02                                          CHAR(24)
 S_DIST_03                                          CHAR(24)
 S_DIST_04                                          CHAR(24)
 S_DIST_05                                          CHAR(24)
 S_DIST_06                                          CHAR(24)
 S_DIST_07                                          CHAR(24)
 S_DIST_08                                          CHAR(24)
 S_DIST_09                                          CHAR(24)
 S_DIST_10                                          CHAR(24)
 S_YTD                                              NUMBER(10)
 S_ORDER_CNT                                        NUMBER(6)
 S_REMOTE_CNT                                       NUMBER(6)
 S_DATA                                             VARCHAR2(50)

Description of C_WAREHOUSE

Name                                      Null?     Type
---------------------------------------- --------- ------------------
 W_ID                                               NUMBER(4)
 W_YTD                                              NUMBER(12,2)
 W_TAX                                              NUMBER(4,4)
 W_NAME                                             VARCHAR2(10)
 W_STREET_1                                         VARCHAR2(20)
 W_STREET_2                                         VARCHAR2(20)
 W_CITY                                             VARCHAR2(20)
 W_STATE                                            CHAR(2)
 W_ZIP                                              CHAR(9)
```

The x_ID columns are the primary keys. Only the primary keys were indexed for the test.

Example AWRRPT

Example AWRRPT Report for 250 Megabyte SGA

The most interesting results were generated by reducing the SGA maximum size from one gigabyte yielding 800 megabyte database caches to 250 megabytes yielding 125 megabyte database caches. In doing so, the amount of data cached was reduced from a virtual 100% to 25%.

This appendix contains the full text, minus the SQL areas, of the AWRRPT report for the SSD test for the 250 Megabyte SGA 600 user run final time frame.

```
WORKLOAD REPOSITORY report for
DB Name         DB Id    Instance     Inst Num Release     Cluster Host
-----------  -----------  -----------  -------- -----------  ------- -----------
SSD          534227347 ssd1               1 10.1.0.3.0  YES     amd41.supers
                Snap Id      Snap Time    Sessions Curs/Sess
             ---------  ------------------- -------- ---------
Begin Snap:        29 29-Jul-05 21:00:52      454        .1
  End Snap:        30 29-Jul-05 22:00:31      478        .1
  Elapsed:              59.66 (mins)
  DB Time:               0.01 (mins)

Cache Sizes (end)
~~~~~~~~~~~~~~~~~
              Buffer Cache:        116M    Std Block Size:       8K
          Shared Pool Size:        120M       Log Buffer:     512K

Load Profile
~~~~~~~~~~~~
                                    Per Second      Per Transaction
                                  ---------------   ---------------
                     Redo size:        607.45          103,543.62
                 Logical reads:         11.54            1,966.33
                 Block changes:          3.41              580.86
                Physical reads:          0.01                0.95
               Physical writes:          0.19               32.81
                    User calls:          0.04                6.86
                       Parses:          0.78              132.52
                  Hard parses:          0.09               15.52
                        Sorts:          0.45               76.24
                       Logons:          0.01                1.33
                      Executes:          1.93              329.33
                  Transactions:          0.01

    % Blocks changed per Read:   29.54    Recursive Call %:    99.83
    Rollback per transaction %:   38.10      Rows per Sort:    13.68

Instance Efficiency Percentages (Target 100%)
~~~~~~~~~~~~~~~~~~~~~~~~~~~~~~~~~~~~~~~~~~~~~~~
           Buffer Nowait %:  100.00      Redo NoWait %:   99.93
```

```
                Buffer  Hit   %:   99.96    In-memory Sort %:  100.00
               Library Hit   %:   89.90      Soft Parse %:   88.29
             Execute to Parse %:   59.76       Latch Hit %:  100.00
    Parse CPU to Parse Elapsd %:   81.32    % Non-Parse CPU:  -73.88

    Shared Pool Statistics        Begin      End
                                  ------    ------
               Memory Usage %:    97.40     97.34
       % SQL with executions>1:   65.50     65.35
       % Memory for SQL w/exec>1: 59.80     61.07

    Top 5 Timed Events
    ~~~~~~~~~~~~~~~~~~~                                  % Total
    Event                            Waits   Time (s)  DB Time   Wait Class
    ------------------------------- -------- --------- --------- --------------
    reliable message                   33        6    1303.84    Other
    class slave wait                    1        5    1120.44    Other
    name-service call wait             36        1     305.37    Other
    control file parallel write     1,174        1     246.92    System I/O
    control file sequential read    3,979        1     221.47    System I/O
                                    ----------------------------------------------


    RAC Statistics  DB/Inst: SSD/ssd1  Snaps: 29-30

                                  Begin    End
                                  -----   -----
             Number of Instances:    2       2


    Global Cache Load Profile
    ~~~~~~~~~~~~~~~~~~~~~~~~~~~                Per Second       Per Transaction
                                             ----------------  ----------------
         Global Cache blocks received:            0.08               13.38
           Global Cache blocks served:            0.09               14.86
            GCS/GES messages received:            2.30              392.19
                GCS/GES messages sent:            2.47              421.48
                   DBWR Fusion writes:            0.02                2.62


    Global Cache Efficiency Percentages (Target local+remote 100%)
    ~~~~~~~~~~~~~~~~~~~~~~~~~~~~~~~~~~~~~~~~~~~~~~~~~~~~~~~~~~~~~~~~~~~
    Buffer access -  local cache %:   99.28
    Buffer access - remote cache %:    0.68
    Buffer access -        disk %:     0.04


    Global Cache and Enqueue Services - Workload Characteristics
    ~~~~~~~~~~~~~~~~~~~~~~~~~~~~~~~~~~~~~~~~~~~~~~~~~~~~~~~~~~~~~~~~
                    Avg global enqueue get time (ms):       0.2

           Avg global cache cr block receive time (ms):     1.0
      Avg global cache current block receive time (ms):     1.0

             Avg global cache cr block build time (ms):     0.0
              Avg global cache cr block send time (ms):     0.1
      Global cache log flushes for cr blocks served %:      0.0
              Avg global cache cr block flush time (ms):

          Avg global cache current block pin time (ms):     0.0
         Avg global cache current block send time (ms):     0.0
    Global cache log flushes for current blocks served %:   0.0
         Avg global cache current block flush time (ms):

    Global Cache and Enqueue Services - Messaging Statistics
    ~~~~~~~~~~~~~~~~~~~~~~~~~~~~~~~~~~~~~~~~~~~~~~~~~~~~~~~~~~~
                    Avg message sent queue time (ms):        0.0
             Avg message sent queue time on ksxp (ms):       0.2
                Avg message received queue time (ms):        0.0
                   Avg GCS message process time (ms):        0.0
                   Avg GES message process time (ms):        0.0

                    % of direct sent messages:             40.48
                    % of indirect sent messages:           45.04
                    % of flow controlled messages:         14.48
                    ----------------------------------------------


    Wait Events  DB/Inst: SSD/ssd1  Snaps: 29-30
    -> s  - second
    -> cs - centisecond -     100th of a second
    -> ms - millisecond -    1000th of a second
    -> us - microsecond - 1000000th of a second
    -> ordered by wait time desc, waits desc (idle events last)
                                                          Avg
                                           Total Wait    wait     Waits
```

Event	Waits	Timeouts	Time (s)	(ms)	/txn
reliable message	33	5	6	176	1.6
class slave wait	1	1	5	4993	0.0
name-service call wait	36	0	1	38	1.7
control file parallel write	1,174	0	1	1	55.9
control file sequential rea	3,979	0	1	0	189.5
process startup	21	0	1	41	1.0
DFS lock handle	2,585	0	1	0	123.1
gc current block 2-way	194	0	0	1	9.2
CGS wait for IPC msg	32,489	32,489	0	0	1,547.1
latch free	5	0	0	33	0.2
log file parallel write	865	0	0	0	41.2
row cache lock	1,099	0	0	0	52.3
gc cr block 2-way	115	0	0	1	5.5
enq: PS - contention	61	0	0	1	2.9
enq: TM - contention	204	0	0	0	9.7
PX qref latch	2	2	0	13	0.1
ksxr poll remote instances	5,301	2,998	0	0	252.4
library cache pin	307	0	0	0	14.6
library cache lock	152	0	0	0	7.2
IPC send completion sync	44	44	0	0	2.1
gc current grant busy	88	0	0	0	4.2
PX Deq: reap credit	2,298	2,283	0	0	109.4
PX Deq: Signal ACK	44	14	0	0	2.1
rdbms ipc reply	106	0	0	0	5.0
gc cr multi block request	4	0	0	1	0.2
db file sequential read	15	0	0	0	0.7
enq: TA - contention	21	0	0	0	1.0
gc current grant 2-way	19	0	0	0	0.9
enq: WF - contention	15	0	0	0	0.7
enq: PI - contention	11	0	0	0	0.5
gc current multi block requ	6	0	0	0	0.3
latch: session allocation	9	0	0	0	0.4
log file sync	2	0	0	1	0.1
db file parallel write	549	0	0	0	26.1
control file single write	3	0	0	0	0.1
enq: HW - contention	5	0	0	0	0.2
enq: DR - contention	4	0	0	0	0.2
enq: AF - task serializatio	3	0	0	0	0.1
enq: JQ - contention	2	0	0	0	0.1
enq: CF - contention	2	0	0	0	0.1
log file single write	2	0	0	0	0.1
enq: TT - contention	1	0	0	0	0.0
log file sequential read	2	0	0	0	0.1
PX Deq Credit: send blkd	4	0	0	0	0.2
direct path write	7	0	0	0	0.3
direct path read	5	0	0	0	0.2
latch: ges resource hash li	1	0	0	0	0.0
LGWR wait for redo copy	1	0	0	0	0.0
gcs remote message	179,574	179,510	6,990	39	8,551.1
PX Idle Wait	1,804	1,780	4,365	2419	85.9
virtual circuit status	120	120	3,517	29307	5.7
gcs remote message	46,500	45,595	3,495	75	2,214.3
Queue Monitor Wait	119	119	3,487	29307	5.7
wakeup time manager	11	0	3,312	301059	0.5
jobq slave wait	14	14	42	3008	0.7
PX Deq: Execution Msg	119	24	0	1	5.7
PX Deq: Msg Fragment	7	1	0	4	0.3
PX Deq: Join ACK	36	10	0	1	1.7
PX Deq: Parse Reply	36	12	0	1	1.7
PX Deq: Execute Reply	30	12	0	0	1.4
Queue Monitor IPC wait	119	119	0	0	5.7

Background Wait Events   DB/Inst: SSD/ssd1   Snaps: 29-30
-> ordered by wait time desc, waits desc (idle events last)

Event	Waits	Timeouts	Total Wait Time (s)	Avg wait (ms)	Waits /txn
class slave wait	1	1	5	4993	0.0
control file parallel write	1,174	0	1	1	55.9
control file sequential rea	3,926	0	1	0	187.0
process startup	21	0	1	41	1.0
DFS lock handle	2,585	0	1	0	123.1
CGS wait for IPC msg	32,489	32,489	0	0	1,547.1
log file parallel write	866	0	0	0	41.2
latch free	4	0	0	25	0.2
gc current block 2-way	60	0	0	1	2.9
gc cr block 2-way	50	0	0	1	2.4
enq: TM - contention	204	0	0	0	9.7
PX qref latch	2	2	0	13	0.1
ksxr poll remote instances	5,303	3,000	0	0	252.5

row cache lock	37	0	0	1	1.8
enq: PS - contention	51	0	0	0	2.4
PX Deq: Signal ACK	44	14	0	0	2.1
reliable message	27	0	0	0	1.3
gc cr multi block request	4	0	0	1	0.2
IPC send completion sync	8	8	0	0	0.4
enq: TA - contention	21	0	0	0	1.0
gc current grant busy	18	0	0	0	0.9
PX Deq: reap credit	284	275	0	0	13.5
db file sequential read	7	0	0	0	0.3
enq: PI - contention	11	0	0	0	0.5
library cache pin	6	0	0	0	0.3
db file parallel write	549	0	0	0	26.1
control file single write	3	0	0	0	0.1
latch: session allocation	4	0	0	0	0.2
enq: DR - contention	4	0	0	0	0.2
rdbms ipc reply	6	0	0	0	0.3
enq: CF - contention	2	0	0	0	0.1
log file single write	2	0	0	0	0.1
log file sequential read	2	0	0	0	0.1
library cache lock	2	0	0	0	0.1
PX Deq Credit: send blkd	4	0	0	0	0.2
direct path read	5	0	0	0	0.2
latch: ges resource hash li	1	0	0	0	0.0
direct path write	5	0	0	0	0.2
LGWR wait for redo copy	1	0	0	0	0.0
rdbms ipc message	47,227	43,863	34,648	734	2,248.9
gcs remote message	179,573	179,509	6,990	39	8,551.1
ges remote message	46,501	45,594	3,495	75	2,214.3
Queue Monitor Wait	119	119	3,487	29307	5.7
wakeup time manager	11	0	3,312	301059	0.5
smon timer	11	11	3,300	299995	0.5
PX Deq: Join ACK	36	10	0	1	1.7
PX Deq: Parse Reply	36	12	0	1	1.7
PX Deq: Execute Reply	30	12	0	0	1.4
Queue Monitor IPC wait	119	119	0	0	5.7

Time Model Statistics DB/Inst: SSD/ssd1 Snaps: 29-30
-> ordered by Time (seconds) desc

Statistic Name	Time (seconds)	% Total DB Time
background elapsed time	26.27	5895.78
background cpu time	12.41	2784.83
DB time	.45	100.00
DB CPU	.43	95.50
sql execute elapsed time	.35	79.25
parse time elapsed	.26	58.26
hard parse elapsed time	.24	52.99
Java execution elapsed time	.05	11.96
PL/SQL execution elapsed time	.03	6.02
PL/SQL compilation elapsed time	.01	2.42
hard parse (sharing criteria) elapsed time	.00	.04
failed parse (out of shared memory) elapsed t	.00	.00
failed parse elapsed time	.00	.00
connection management call elapsed time	.00	.00
hard parse (bind mismatch) elapsed time	.00	.00
inbound PL/SQL rpc elapsed time	.00	.00
sequence load elapsed time	.00	.28

Operating System Statistics DB/Inst: SSD/ssd1 Snaps: 29-30

Statistic Name	Value
AVG_BUSY_TICKS	7,757
AVG_IDLE_TICKS	346,964
AVG_IN_BYTES	474,820,608
AVG_NICE_TICKS	1,677
AVG_OUT_BYTES	239,495,168
AVG_SYS_TICKS	2,180
AVG_USER_TICKS	3,900
BUSY_TICKS	15,514
IDLE_TICKS	693,927
IN_BYTES	949,641,216
NICE_TICKS	3,354
OUT_BYTES	478,990,336
RSRC_MGR_CPU_WAIT_TIME	0
SYS_TICKS	4,359
USER_TICKS	7,801

```
Service Statistics  DB/Inst: SSD/ssd1  Snaps: 29-30
-> ordered by DB Time

                                                   Physical   Logical
Service Name                 DB Time (s)  DB CPU (s)   Reads     Reads
---------------------------  -----------  ----------  --------  --------
SYS$USERS                        0.4          0.4          0     4,216
SYS$BACKGROUND                   0.1          0.1         14    37,061
ssd                              0.0          0.0          0         0
ssdXDB                           0.0          0.0          0         0
         -----------------------------------------------------------------

Service Wait Class Stats  DB/Inst: SSD/ssd1  Snaps: 29-30
-> Wait Class info for services in the Service Statistics section.
-> Total Waits and Time Waited displayed for the following wait
   classes:  User I/O, Concurrency, Administrative, Network
-> Time Waited (Wt Time) in centisecond (100th of a second)

Service Name
----------------------------------------------------------------------
User I/O  User I/O  Concurcy  Concurcy   Admin     Admin    Network   Network
Total Wts  Wt Time Total Wts  Wt Time Total Wts  Wt Time Total Wts   Wt Time
---------  -------- ---------  -------- ---------  -------- ---------  ---------
SYS$USERS
       0        0      139        2        0         0        0         0
SYS$BACKGROUND
   63132        0     1453       14        0         0        1         0
ssd
       0        0        0        0        0         0        0         0
         -----------------------------------------------------------------

Instance Activity Stats  DB/Inst: SSD/ssd1  Snaps: 29-30
Statistic                                 Total    per Second   per Trans
-------------------------------  ------------------  ----------  ----------
CPU used by this session                     40         0.0        1.9
CPU used when call started                   40         0.0        1.9
CR blocks created                             0         0.0        0.0
Cached Commit SCN referenced                  0         0.0        0.0
Commit SCN cached                             0         0.0        0.0
DB time                                   6,216         1.7      296.0
DBWR checkpoint buffers written             639         0.2       30.4
DBWR checkpoints                              1         0.0        0.1
DBWR fusion writes                           55         0.0        2.6
DBWR thread checkpoint buffers w              0         0.0        0.0
DBWR transaction table writes               179         0.1        8.5
DBWR undo block writes                      273         0.1       13.0
DFO trees parallelized                       12         0.0        0.6
IPC CPU used by this session                392         0.1       18.7
PX local messages recv'd                     54         0.0        2.6
PX local messages sent                       54         0.0        2.6
PX remote messages recv'd                    54         0.0        2.6
PX remote messages sent                      54         0.0        2.6
Parallel operations downgraded t              2         0.0        0.1
Parallel operations not downgrad             12         0.0        0.6
SQL*Net roundtrips to/from clien              0         0.0        0.0
active txn count during cleanout             39         0.0        1.9
application wait time                         1         0.0        0.1
background checkpoints completed              1         0.0        0.1
background checkpoints started                1         0.0        0.1
background timeouts                       11,177        3.1      532.2
branch node splits                            0         0.0        0.0
buffer is not pinned count               18,271        5.1      870.1
buffer is pinned count                    4,533        1.3      215.9
bytes received via SQL*Net from               0         0.0        0.0
bytes sent via SQL*Net to client              0         0.0        0.0
calls to get snapshot scn: kcmgs         10,086        2.8      480.3
calls to kcmgas                             782         0.2       37.2
calls to kcmgcs                              40         0.0        1.9
change write time                             7         0.0        0.3
cleanout - number of ktugct call             43         0.0        2.1
cleanouts and rollbacks - consis              0         0.0        0.0
cleanouts only - consistent read              0         0.0        0.0
cluster key scan block gets               1,614        0.5       76.9
cluster key scans                           732         0.2       34.9
cluster wait time                            29         0.0        1.4
commit cleanout failures: callba              0         0.0        0.0
commit cleanout failures: cannot              0         0.0        0.0
commit cleanouts                            515         0.1       24.5
commit cleanouts successfully co            515         0.1       24.5
commit txn count during cleanout             23         0.0        1.1
concurrency wait time                        13         0.0        0.6
consistent changes                            0         0.0        0.0
consistent gets                          29,486        8.2    1,404.1
consistent gets - examination            11,402        3.2      543.0
consistent gets from cache               29,486        8.2    1,404.1
current blocks converted for CR               0         0.0        0.0
```

Example AWRRPT Report for 250 Megabyte SGA　　**185**

```
cursor authentications                  71          0.0          3.4
data blocks consistent reads - u          0          0.0          0.0
db block changes                     12,198          3.4        580.9
db block gets                        11,807          3.3        562.2
db block gets direct                      6          0.0          0.3
db block gets from cache             11,801          3.3        562.0
```

Instance Activity Stats DB/Inst: SSD/ssd1 Snaps: 29-30

Statistic	Total	per Second	per Trans
deferred (CURRENT) block cleanou	315	0.1	15.0
dirty buffers inspected	0	0.0	0.0
enqueue conversions	760	0.2	36.2
enqueue releases	33,946	9.5	1,616.5
enqueue requests	33,957	9.5	1,617.0
enqueue timeouts	11	0.0	0.5
enqueue waits	228	0.1	10.9
exchange deadlocks	0	0.0	0.0
execute count	6,916	1.9	329.3
frame signature mismatch	0	0.0	0.0
free buffer inspected	274	0.1	13.1
free buffer requested	393	0.1	18.7
gc CPU used by this session	429	0.1	20.4
gc blocks lost	0	0.0	0.0
gc cr block build time	0	0.0	0.0
gc cr block flush time	0	0.0	0.0
gc cr block receive time	11	0.0	0.5
gc cr block send time	1	0.0	0.1
gc cr blocks received	107	0.0	5.1
gc cr blocks served	143	0.0	6.8
gc current block flush time	0	0.0	0.0
gc current block pin time	0	0.0	0.0
gc current block receive time	17	0.0	0.8
gc current block send time	0	0.0	0.0
gc current blocks received	174	0.1	8.3
gc current blocks served	169	0.1	8.1
gcs messages sent	611	0.2	29.1
ges messages sent	8,240	2.3	392.4
global enqueue CPU used by this	152	0.0	7.2
global enqueue get time	157	0.0	7.5
global enqueue gets async	2,314	0.7	110.2
global enqueue gets sync	4,435	1.2	211.2
global enqueue releases	5,359	1.5	255.2
heap block compress	21	0.0	1.0
hot buffers moved to head of LRU	56	0.0	2.7
immediate (CR) block cleanout ap	0	0.0	0.0
immediate (CURRENT) block cleano	35	0.0	1.7
index fetch by key	3,934	1.1	187.3
index scans kdiixs1	4,628	1.3	220.4
leaf node 90-10 splits	11	0.0	0.5
leaf node splits	14	0.0	0.7
logons cumulative	28	0.0	1.3
messages received	3,373	0.9	160.6
messages sent	3,373	0.9	160.6
no buffer to keep pinned count	0	0.0	0.0
no work - consistent read gets	11,847	3.3	564.1
opened cursors cumulative	2,499	0.7	119.0
parse count (failures)	2	0.0	0.1
parse count (hard)	326	0.1	15.5
parse count (total)	2,783	0.8	132.5
parse time cpu	74	0.0	3.5
parse time elapsed	91	0.0	4.3
physical read IO requests	20	0.0	1.0
physical reads	20	0.0	1.0
physical reads cache	15	0.0	0.7
physical reads direct	5	0.0	0.2
physical write IO requests	569	0.2	27.1

Instance Activity Stats DB/Inst: SSD/ssd1 Snaps: 29-30

Statistic	Total	per Second	per Trans
physical writes	689	0.2	32.8
physical writes direct	11	0.0	0.5
physical writes from cache	678	0.2	32.3
physical writes non checkpoint	215	0.1	10.2
pinned buffers inspected	0	0.0	0.0
prefetch clients - default	0	0.0	0.0
prefetch warmup blocks aged out	0	0.0	0.0
prefetched blocks aged out befor	0	0.0	0.0
process last non-idle time	28,067,180,613	7,840,956.1	#############
queries parallelized	12	0.0	0.6
recursive calls	86,545	24.2	4,121.2

```
recursive cpu usage                        258             0.1          12.3
redo blocks written                      4,957             1.4         236.1
redo buffer allocation retries              35             0.0           1.7
redo entries                             7,339             2.1         349.5
redo log space requests                      5             0.0           0.2
redo log space wait time                     0             0.0           0.0
redo ordering marks                         87             0.0           4.1
redo size                            2,174,416           607.5     103,543.6
redo synch time                              0             0.0           0.0
redo synch writes                            4             0.0           0.2
redo wastage                           313,276            87.5      14,917.9
redo write time                              8             0.0           0.4
redo writer latching time                    0             0.0           0.0
redo writes                                866             0.2          41.2
rollback changes - undo records              2             0.0           0.1
rollbacks only - consistent read             0             0.0           0.0
rows fetched via callback                2,150             0.6         102.4
session connect time            28,067,180,613     7,840,956.1 #############
session logical reads                   41,293            11.5       1,966.3
session pga memory                  12,227,968         3,416.1     582,284.2
session pga memory max              12,293,504         3,434.4     585,405.0
session uga memory                     850,560           237.6      40,502.9
session uga memory max               9,065,004         2,532.4     431,666.9
shared hash latch upgrades - no          4,464             1.3         212.6
shared hash latch upgrades - wai             0             0.0           0.0
sorts (memory)                           1,601             0.5          76.2
sorts (rows)                            21,903             6.1       1,043.0
summed dirty queue length                    0             0.0           0.0
switch current to new buffer                 0             0.0           0.0
table fetch by rowid                     8,400             2.4         400.0
table fetch continued row                  142             0.0           6.8
table scan blocks gotten                 2,275             0.6         108.3
table scan rows gotten                  18,564             5.2         884.0
table scans (long tables)                    0             0.0           0.0
table scans (short tables)                 832             0.2          39.6
transaction lock foreground requ             0             0.0           0.0
transaction lock foreground wait             0             0.0           0.0
transaction rollbacks                        1             0.0           0.1
undo change vector size                650,440           181.7      30,973.3
user calls                                 144             0.0           6.9
user commits                                13             0.0           0.6
user rollbacks                               8             0.0           0.4
workarea executions - optimal              645             0.2          30.7
write clones created in backgrou             0             0.0           0.0
write clones created in foregrou             0             0.0           0.0
          -------------------------------------------------------------------
```

Instance Activity Stats - Absolute Values DB/Inst: SSD/ssd1 Snaps: 29-30
-> Statistics with absolute values (should not be diffed)
-> Statistics identified by '(derived)' come from sources other than SYSSTAT

```
Statistic                         Begin Value      End Value
-------------------------------- --------------- ---------------
logons current                            454             478
open threads (derived)                      4               4
opened cursors current                     61              61
          -------------------------------------------------------------------
```

Instance Activity Stats - Thread Activity DB/Inst: SSD/ssd1 Snaps: 29-30

```
Statistic                              Total  per Hour
-------------------------------- ------------------ ---------
log switches (derived)                     1      1.01
          -------------------------------------------------------------------
```

Tablespace IO Stats DB/Inst: SSD/ssd1 Snaps: 29-30
-> ordered by IOs (Reads + Writes) desc

Tablespace

	Reads	Av Reads/s	Av Rd(ms)	Av Blks/Rd	Writes	Av Writes/s	Buffer Waits	Av Buf Wt(ms)
UNDOTBS1	2	0	0.0	1.0	372	0	0	0.0
SYSAUX	7	0	0.0	1.0	136	0	0	0.0
SYSTEM	3	0	0.0	1.0	59	0	0	0.0
UNDOTBS2	1	0	0.0	1.0	1	0	0	0.0
USERS	1	0	0.0	1.0	1	0	0	0.0

Example AWRRPT Report for 250 Megabyte SGA   **187**

```
File IO Stats  DB/Inst: SSD/ssd1  Snaps: 29-30
-> ordered by Tablespace, File

Tablespace                  Filename
-----------------------     -------------------------------------------------
                 Av    Av    Av                          Av   Buffer Av Buf
       Reads Reads/s Rd(ms) Blks/Rd      Writes Writes/s Waits Wt(ms)
------------- ------- ------ ------- ------------- -------- ---------- ------
SYSAUX                      /oracle2/oradata/ssd/sysaux01.dbf
          7      0    0.0    1.0         136      0            0    0.0
SYSTEM                      /oracle2/oradata/ssd/system01.dbf
          3      0    0.0    1.0          59      0            0    0.0
UNDOTBS1                    /oracle2/oradata/ssd/undotbs01.dbf
          2      0    0.0    1.0         372      0            0    0.0
UNDOTBS2                    /oracle2/oradata/ssd/undotbs02.dbf
          1      0    0.0    1.0           1      0            0    0.0
USERS                       /oracle2/oradata/ssd/users01.dbf
          1      0    0.0    1.0           1      0            0    0.0
                           -------------------------------------------------


Buffer Pool Statistics  DB/Inst: SSD/ssd1  Snaps: 29-30
-> Standard block size Pools  D: default,  K: keep,  R: recycle
-> Default Pools for other block sizes: 2k, 4k, 8k, 16k, 32k

                                                      Free Writ    Buffer
    Number of Pool           Buffer    Physical  Physical Buff Comp   Busy
P    Buffers Hit%             Gets       Reads    Writes Wait Wait   Waits
--- --------- ---- --------------- ------------ ---------- ---- ---- ----------
D    14,210  100          41,255           12       678    0    0            0
                   -------------------------------------------------------------


Instance Recovery Stats  DB/Inst: SSD/ssd1  Snaps: 29-30
-> B: Begin snapshot,  E: End snapshot

   Targt Estd                                 Log File Log Ckpt   Log Ckpt
   MTTR  MTTR                                     Size  Timeout   Interval
   (s)   (s)  Estd IOs Redo Blks Redo Blks Redo Blks Redo Blks Redo Blks
 - ----- ----- --------- --------- --------- --------- --------- ------------
B    0    13       258      2143      1299      18432      1299
E    0    13       232      2138       505      18432       505
                 ------------------------------------------------------------


Buffer Pool Advisory  DB/Inst: SSD/ssd1  Snap: 30
-> Only rows with estimated physical reads >0 are displayed
-> ordered by Block Size, Buffers For Estimate

      Size for  Size       Buffers for Est Physical       Estimated
P   Estimate (M) Factr       Estimate  Read Factor   Physical Reads
--- ------------ ----- ----------------- ------------- -------------------
D            8    .1              980        92.13      126,422,382
D           16    .1            1,960        56.22       77,151,118
D           24    .2            2,940        18.38       25,217,065
D           32    .3            3,920         9.59       13,161,157
D           40    .3            4,900         4.93        6,770,909
D           48    .4            5,880         3.22        4,418,125
D           56    .5            6,860         2.60        3,570,456
D           64    .6            7,840         2.15        2,946,769
D           72    .6            8,820         1.83        2,515,036
D           80    .7            9,800         1.61        2,209,522
D           88    .8           10,780         1.42        1,954,215
D           96    .8           11,760         1.27        1,749,440
D          104    .9           12,740         1.16        1,585,998
D          112   1.0           13,720         1.05        1,438,408
D          116   1.0           14,210         1.00        1,372,241
D          120   1.0           14,700         0.95        1,304,938
D          128   1.1           15,680         0.88        1,207,122
D          136   1.2           16,660         0.82        1,122,020
D          144   1.2           17,640         0.77        1,051,146
D          152   1.3           18,620         0.72          992,500
D          160   1.4           19,600         0.69          941,806
                 ------------------------------------------------------------


PGA Aggr Summary  DB/Inst: SSD/ssd1  Snaps: 29-30
-> PGA cache hit % - percentage of W/A (WorkArea) data processed only in-memory

PGA Cache Hit %  W/A MB Processed  Extra W/A MB Read/Written
--------------- ----------------- --------------------------
        100.0              11                         0
                 ------------------------------------------------------------

PGA Aggr Target Stats  DB/Inst: SSD/ssd1  Snaps: 29-30
-> B: Begin snap   E: End snap (rows dentified with B or E contain data
```

```
           which is absolute i.e. not diffed over the interval)
-> Auto PGA Target  - actual workarea memory target
-> W/A PGA Used     - amount of memory used for all Workareas (manual + auto)
-> %PGA W/A Mem     - percentage of PGA memory allocated to workareas
-> %Auto W/A Mem    - percentage of workarea memory controlled by Auto Mem Mgmt
-> %Man W/A Mem     - percentage of workarea memory under manual control
```

	PGA Aggr Target(M)	Auto PGA Target(M)	PGA Mem Alloc(M)	W/A PGA Used(M)	%PGA W/A Mem	%Auto W/A Mem	%Man W/A Mem	Global Mem Bound(K)
B	340	275	94.3	0.0	.0	.0	.0	17,408
E	340	274	94.3	0.0	.0	.0	.0	17,408

```
PGA Aggr Target Histogram  DB/Inst: SSD/ssd1  Snaps: 29-30
-> Optimal Executions are purely in-memory operations
```

Low Optimal	High Optimal	Total Execs	Optimal Execs	1-Pass Execs	M-Pass Execs
2K	4K	631	631	0	0
256K	512K	2	2	0	0
512K	1024K	12	12	0	0

```
PGA Memory Advisory  DB/Inst: SSD/ssd1  Snap: 30
-> When using Auto Memory Mgmt, minimally choose a pga_aggregate_target value
   where Estd PGA Overalloc Count is 0
```

PGA Target Est (MB)	Size Factr	W/A MB Processed	Estd Extra W/A MB Read/ Written to Disk	Estd PGA Cache Hit %	Estd PGA Overalloc Count
43	0.1	18,354.1	11,000.7	63.0	460
85	0.3	18,354.1	10,389.0	64.0	420
170	0.5	18,354.1	6,525.0	74.0	205
255	0.8	18,354.1	0.0	100.0	0
340	1.0	18,354.1	0.0	100.0	0
408	1.2	18,354.1	0.0	100.0	0
476	1.4	18,354.1	0.0	100.0	0
544	1.6	18,354.1	0.0	100.0	0
612	1.8	18,354.1	0.0	100.0	0
680	2.0	18,354.1	0.0	100.0	0
1,020	3.0	18,354.1	0.0	100.0	0
1,360	4.0	18,354.1	0.0	100.0	0
2,040	6.0	18,354.1	0.0	100.0	0
2,720	8.0	18,354.1	0.0	100.0	0

```
Shared Pool Advisory  DB/Inst: SSD/ssd1  Snap: 30
-> SP: Shared Pool    Est LC: Estimated Library Cache    Factr: Factor
-> Note there is often a 1:Many correlation between a single logical object
   in the Library Cache, and the physical number of memory objects associated
   with it.  Therefore comparing the number of Lib Cache objects (e.g. in
   v$librarycache), with the number of Lib Cache Memory Objects is invalid.
```

Shared Pool Size(M)	SP Size Factr	Est LC Size (M)	Est LC Mem Obj	Est LC Time Saved (s)	Est LC Time Saved Factr	Est LC Load Time (s)	Est LC Load Time Factr	Est LC Mem Obj Hits
108	.9	12	2,040	119	1.0	51	1.0	52,242
120	1.0	23	4,266	119	1.0	51	1.0	52,954
132	1.1	34	6,021	119	1.0	51	1.0	52,973
144	1.2	43	7,454	119	1.0	51	1.0	52,981
156	1.3	43	7,454	119	1.0	51	1.0	52,981
168	1.4	43	7,454	119	1.0	51	1.0	52,981
180	1.5	43	7,454	119	1.0	51	1.0	52,981
192	1.6	43	7,454	119	1.0	51	1.0	52,981
204	1.7	43	7,454	119	1.0	51	1.0	52,981
216	1.8	43	7,454	119	1.0	51	1.0	52,981
228	1.9	43	7,454	119	1.0	51	1.0	52,981
240	2.0	43	7,454	119	1.0	51	1.0	52,981

```
Java Pool Advisory  DB/Inst: SSD/ssd1  Snap: 30
```

Java Pool Size(M)	JP Size Factr	Est LC Size (M)	Est LC Mem Obj	Est LC Time Saved (s)	Est LC Time Saved Factr	Est LC Load Time (s)	Est LC Load Time Factr	Est LC Mem Obj Hits
4	.5	4	45	0	.0	23	1.0	31
8	1.0	4	45	0	.0	23	1.0	31

Example AWRRPT Report for 250 Megabyte SGA   **189**

```
        12   1.5        4          45          0     .0        23    1.0          31
        16   2.0        4          45          0     .0        23    1.0          31
        --------------------------------------------------------------------
```

Buffer Wait Statistics DB/Inst: SSD/ssd1 Snaps: 29-30

                    No data exists for this section of the report.

Enqueue Activity DB/Inst: SSD/ssd1 Snaps: 29-30
-> Enqueue stats gathered prior to 10i should not be compared with 10i data
-> ordered by Wait Time desc, Waits desc

Enqueue Type (Request Reason)

    Requests   Succ Gets Failed Gets   Waits Wt Time (s) Av Wt Time(ms)
------------ ------------ ----------- ----------- ------------ ---------------
TM-DML
        388   388   0   159   0   .44
PS-PX Process Reservation
        119   108   11   37   0   .54
PI-Remote PX Process Spawn Status
         16   16   0   6   0   1.67
TA-Instance Undo
         11   11   0   11   0   .00
WF-SWRF Flush
         11   11   0   10   0   .00
HW-Segment High Water Mark
        919   919   0   3   0   .00
DR-Distributed Recovery
          2   2   0   2   0   .00
AF-Advisor Framework (task serialization)
          7   7   0   1   0   .00
JQ-Job Queue
          1   1   0   1   0   .00
TT-Tablespace
         71   71   0   1   0   .00
CF-Controlfile Transaction
      5,078   5,078   0   1   0   .00

Undo Segment Summary DB/Inst: SSD/ssd1 Snaps: 29-30
-> Undo segment block stats:
-> uS - unexpired Stolen,   uR - unexpired Released,   uU - unexpired reUsed
-> eS - expired   Stolen,   eR - expired   Released,   eU - expired   reUsed

Undo   Undo   Num Max Qry Max Tx Snap OutOf   uS/uR/uU/
TS#   Blocks   Trans Len (s) Concurcy TooOld Space   eS/eR/eU
--- ------------ ---------------- -------- -------- ------ ----- ---------------
  1   94   328   0   3   0   0 0/0/0/0/0/0

Undo Segment Stats DB/Inst: SSD/ssd1 Snaps: 29-30
-> ordered by Time desc

                Undo   Num Max Qry Max Tx Snap OutOf   uS/uR/uU/
End Time   Blocks   Trans Len (s) Concy TooOld Space   eS/eR/eU
----------- ------------ ------------- ------- -------- ------ ----- ----------------
29-Jul 21:55   0   5   0   0   0   0 0/0/0/0/0/0
29-Jul 21:45   0   2   0   0   0   0 0/0/0/0/0/0
29-Jul 21:35   4   23   0   1   0   0 0/0/0/0/0/0
29-Jul 21:25   0   12   0   0   0   0 0/0/0/0/0/0
29-Jul 21:15   0   3   0   0   0   0 0/0/0/0/0/0
29-Jul 21:05   90   283   0   3   0   0 0/0/0/0/0/0

Latch Activity DB/Inst: SSD/ssd1 Snaps: 29-30
-> "Get Requests", "Pct Get Miss" and "Avg Slps/Miss" are statistics for
   willing-to-wait latch get requests
-> "NoWait Requests", "Pct NoWait Miss" are for no-wait latch get requests
-> "Pct Misses" for both should be very close to 0.0

                               Pct   Avg   Wait   Pct
                        Get   Get   Slps   Time   NoWait NoWait
Latch Name   Requests   Miss /Miss   (s)   Requests Miss
-------------------- --------------- ------ ------ ------ ------------ ------
Consistent RBA   868   0.0   0   0
FOB s.o list latch   25   0.0   0   0
JOX SGA heap latch   883   0.0   0   0
JS broadcast add buf lat 1,497   0.0   0   0
JS broadcast drop buf la 798   0.0   0   0
JS queue state obj latch 25,164 0.0   0   0
JS slv state obj latch   3   0.0   0   0
```
```

```
KCL gc element parent la        3,475    0.0              0         0
KJC message pool free li        1,022    0.0              0        49    0.0
KJCT flow control latch        14,458    0.0              0         0
KSXR large replies                  1    0.0              0         0
KTF sga enqueue                    22    0.0              0     1,158    0.0
KWQMN job cache list lat          130    0.0              0         0
KWQMN job instance list           119    0.0              0         0
MQL Tracking Latch                  0                     0        71    0.0
Memory Management Latch        17,430    0.0              0     1,163    0.0
PL/SQL warning settings            44    0.0              0         0
SQL memory manager latch            1    0.0              0     1,162    0.0
SQL memory manager worka       78,213    0.0              0         0
SWRF Alerted Metric Elem       11,648    0.0              0         0
active checkpoint queue         1,739    0.0              0         0
active service list             5,872    0.0              0         0
begin backup scn array              1    0.0              0         0
business card                      24    0.0              0         0
cache buffer handles               10    0.0              0         0
cache buffers chains           96,725    0.0              0       430    0.0
cache buffers lru chain         1,994    0.0              0     8,486    0.0
channel handle pool latc           32    0.0              0         0
channel operations paren      131,748    0.0              0         0
checkpoint queue latch         26,160    0.0              0       525    0.0
child cursor hash table         3,531    0.0              0         0
client/application info             2    0.0              0         0
compile environment latc           75    0.0              0         0
cursor bind value captur          147    0.0              0        77    0.0
dml lock allocation               827    0.0              0         0
dummy allocation                   80    0.0              0         0
enqueue hash chains            71,755    0.0        0.0    0         0
enqueues                       66,597    0.0        0.0    0         0
error message lists                60    0.0              0         0
event group latch                  15    0.0              0         0
file cache latch                  240    0.0              0         0
gcs opaque info freelist          348    0.0              0         0
gcs resource freelist             155    0.0              0         0
gcs resource hash               2,572    0.0              0         0
gcs shadows freelist              160    0.0              0         0
ges caches resource list        5,679    0.0        0.0    0    35,639    0.0
ges deadlock list                 146    0.0              0         0
ges domain table                2,934    0.0              0         0
ges enqueue table freeli       15,906    0.0        0.0    0         0
ges group table                 8,441    0.0              0         0
ges process hash list           2,637    0.0              0         0
ges process parent latch       27,632    0.0              0         0
ges process table freeli           30    0.0              0         0
ges resource hash list         31,756    0.0        0.5    0     3,666    0.0
ges resource scan list             15    0.0              0         0
ges resource table freel       11,400    0.0              0         0
ges timeout list                  682    0.0              0       711    0.0
hash table column usage           316    0.0              0     2,122    0.0
hash table modification            54    0.0              0         0
job workq parent latch              0                     0         2    0.0
```

Latch Activity DB/Inst: SSD/ssd1 Snaps: 29-30
-> "Get Requests", "Pct Get Miss" and "Avg Slps/Miss" are statistics for
   willing-to-wait latch get requests
-> "NoWait Requests", "Pct NoWait Miss" are for no-wait latch get requests
-> "Pct Misses" for both should be very close to 0.0

Latch Name	Get Requests	Pct Get Miss	Avg Slps /Miss	Wait Time (s)	NoWait Requests	Pct NoWait Miss
job_queue_processes para	61	0.0		0	0	
ksuosstats global area	241	0.0		0	0	
ksxp tid allocation	334	0.0		0	0	
ktm global data	11	0.0		0	0	
lgwr LWN SCN	1,440	0.0		0	0	
library cache	51,530	0.0	0.0	0	1,658	0.0
library cache load lock	1,796	0.0		0	0	
library cache lock	15,984	0.0		0	0	
library cache lock alloc	272	0.0		0	0	
library cache pin	30,258	0.0		0	0	
library cache pin alloca	272	0.0		0	0	
list of block allocation	14	0.0		0	0	
loader state object free	14	0.0		0	0	
message pool operations	153	0.0		0	0	
messages	98,839	0.0	0.0	0	0	
mostly latch-free SCN	1,440	0.0		0	0	
multiblock read objects	4	0.0		0	0	
name-service memory obje	410	0.2	0.0	0	0	
name-service namespace b	33,147	0.0		0	0	
name-service namespace o	12	0.0		0	0	
name-service pending que	230	0.0		0	0	

```
name-service request           72    0.0              0              0
name-service request que   32,803    0.0              0              0
ncodef allocation latch        57    0.0              0              0
object queue header oper    20,300    0.0              0              0
object stats modificatio       93    0.0              0              0
parallel query alloc buf      824    0.0              0              0
parallel query stats           60    0.0              0              0
parameter table allocati       80    0.0              0              0
post/wait queue                 3    0.0              0              2    0.0
process allocation         32,645    0.0              0             15    0.0
process group creation         30    0.0              0              0
process queue                 192    0.0              0              0
process queue reference     2,589    0.0              0            234   17.9
query server freelists        156    0.0              0              0
query server process           12   33.3    1.0       0             12    0.0
redo allocation             3,791    0.0    0.0       0          7,398    0.0
redo copy                       0                     0          7,399    0.0
redo writing                6,785    0.0              0              0
row cache objects          61,350    0.0    0.0       0          1,348    0.0
sequence cache                118    0.0              0              0
session allocation        145,580    0.0    0.8       0              0
session idle bit              347    0.0              0              0
session switching              57    0.0              0              0
session timer               1,196    0.0              0              0
shared pool                49,635    0.0    0.0       0              0
simulator hash latch        3,804    0.0              0              0
simulator lru latch            23    0.0              0             51    0.0
slave class                     2    0.0              0              0
slave class create              8   12.5    1.0       0              0
sort extent pool              104    0.0              0              0
state object free list          2    0.0              0              0
statistics aggregation        140    0.0              0              0
threshold alerts latch        130    0.0              0              0
transaction allocation         10    0.0              0              0
transaction branch alloc       57    0.0              0              0
undo global data            4,989    0.0              0              0
user lock                       3    0.0              0              0
          -------------------------------------------------------------
```

Latch Sleep Breakdown   DB/Inst: SSD/ssd1   Snaps: 29-30
-> ordered by misses desc

Latch Name

Get Requests	Misses	Sleeps	Spin Gets	Sleep1	Sleep2	Sleep3
session allocation						
145,580	11	9	2	9	0	0
query server process						
12	4	4	0	4	0	0
ges resource hash list						
31,756	2	1	1	1	0	0
slave class create						
8	1	1	0	1	0	0

Latch Miss Sources   DB/Inst: SSD/ssd1   Snaps: 29-30
-> only latches with sleeps are shown
-> ordered by name, sleeps desc

Latch Name	Where	NoWait Misses	Sleeps	Waiter Sleeps
ges resource hash list	kjlrlr: remove lock from r	0	1	0
query server process	kxfpcrer	0	4	0
session allocation	ksuxds: KSUSFCLC not set	0	7	3
session allocation	ksursi	0	2	2
slave class create	ksvcreate	0	1	0

Parent Latch Statistics   DB/Inst: SSD/ssd1   Snaps: 29-30

                    No data exists for this section of the report.

Child Latch Statistics   DB/Inst: SSD/ssd1   Snaps: 29-30

                    No data exists for this section of the report.

Segments by Logical Reads   DB/Inst: SSD/ssd1   Snaps: 29-30
-> % Total shows % of logical reads for each top segment compared with total

Oracle RAC & Grid Tuning with SSD

```
                logical reads for all segments captured by the Snapshot

             Tablespace                        Subobject  Obj.     Logical
  Owner      Name       Object Name             Name       Type       Reads  %Total
  ---------- ---------- --------------------    ---------- -----  ---------- ------
  SYS        SYSTEM     I_HH_OBJ#_INTCOL#                  INDEX      2,976   8.17
  SYS        SYSTEM     JOB$                               TABLE      2,192   6.02
  SYS        SYSTEM     I_CCOL1                            INDEX      1,632   4.48
  SYS        SYSTEM     I_OBJ#                             INDEX        960   2.64
  SYS        SYSTEM     I_OBJ1                             INDEX        912   2.50
             -----------------------------------------------------------------

  Segments by Physical Reads  DB/Inst: SSD/ssd1  Snaps: 29-30

             Tablespace                        Subobject  Obj.     Physical
  Owner      Name       Object Name             Name       Type       Reads  %Total
  ---------- ---------- --------------------    ---------- -----  ---------- ------
  SYS        SYSTEM     SMON_SCN_TIME                      TABLE          2  25.00
  SYS        SYSAUX     WRH$_SQLBIND            34227347_0 TABLE          2  25.00
  SYS        SYSAUX     WRI$_SCH_CONTROL                   TABLE          1  12.50
  SYS        SYSAUX     WRM$_SNAPSHOT_PK                   INDEX          1  12.50
  SYS        SYSAUX     WRH$_ACTIVE_SESSION_    34227347_0 INDEX          1  12.50
             -----------------------------------------------------------------


  Segments by Buffer Busy Waits  DB/Inst: SSD/ssd1  Snaps: 29-30

                    No data exists for this section of the report.
             -----------------------------------------------------------------

  Segments by Row Lock Waits  DB/Inst: SSD/ssd1  Snaps: 29-30

                                                           Row
             Tablespace                        Subobject  Obj.      Lock
  Owner      Name       Object Name             Name       Type     Waits  %Total
  ---------- ---------- --------------------    ---------- -----  ------------ ------
  SYS        SYSTEM     SMON_SCN_TIME                      TABLE         2 100.00
             -----------------------------------------------------------------

  Segments by ITL Waits  DB/Inst: SSD/ssd1  Snaps: 29-30

                    No data exists for this section of the report.
             -----------------------------------------------------------------

  Segments by CR Blocks Received  DB/Inst: SSD/ssd1  Snaps: 29-30

                                                           CR
             Tablespace                        Subobject  Obj.     Blocks
  Owner      Name       Object Name             Name       Type   Received  %Total
  ---------- ---------- --------------------    ---------- -----  ------------ ------
  SYS        SYSTEM     SMON_SCN_TIME                      TABLE         25  22.12
  SYS        SYSTEM     SEG$                               TABLE         22  19.47
  SYS        SYSTEM     SMON_SCN_TIME_TIM_ID               INDEX         10   8.85
  SYS        SYSTEM     CACHE_STATS_1$                     TABLE         10   8.85
  SYS        SYSTEM     SEQ$                               TABLE          5   4.42
             -----------------------------------------------------------------

  Segments by Current Blocks Received  DB/Inst: SSD/ssd1  Snaps: 29-30

                                                          Current
             Tablespace                        Subobject  Obj.     Blocks
  Owner      Name       Object Name             Name       Type   Received  %Total
  ---------- ---------- --------------------    ---------- -----  ------------ ------
  SYS        SYSTEM     COL_USAGE$                         TABLE         15   8.67
  SYS        SYSTEM     SMON_SCN_TIME                      TABLE         12   6.94
  SYS        SYSTEM     SMON_SCN_TIME_TIM_ID               INDEX         10   5.78
  SYS        SYSTEM     CACHE_STATS_1$                     TABLE         10   5.78
  SYS        SYSTEM     SMON_SCN_TIME_SCN_ID               INDEX         10   5.78
             -----------------------------------------------------------------

  Dictionary Cache Stats  DB/Inst: SSD/ssd1  Snaps: 29-30
  -> "Pct Misses"  should be very low (< 2% in most cases)
  -> "Final Usage" is the number of cache entries being used

                              Get    Pct   Scan   Pct     Mod    Final
  Cache                   Requests   Miss  Reqs   Miss    Reqs    Usage
  --------------------   --------- ------ ------ ------ -------- ---------
  dc_awr_control               63    0.0      0                2         1
  dc_global_oids              900    0.7      0                0        16
  dc_histogram_data           241   14.5      0                0        80
  dc_histogram_defs         2,481   59.5      0                0     1,044
  dc_object_ids             2,658    2.7      0                0       357
  dc_objects                1,205   13.6      0                0       352
  dc_profiles                   1  100.0      0                0         1
```

Example AWRRPT Report for 250 Megabyte SGA **193**

```
dc_rollback_segments        5,015    0.0      0             0      273
dc_segments                   476    31.3      0             0      162
dc_sequences                   47    10.6      0            47        1
dc_tablespaces                882     0.0      0             0        6
dc_usernames                  226     0.0      0             0        4
dc_users                    1,455     0.0      0             0        3
outstanding_alerts             36    66.7      0             0        5
                  -------------------------------------------------------
```

```
Dictionary Cache Stats (RAC)  DB/Inst: SSD/ssd1  Snaps: 29-30

                              GES          GES          GES
Cache                     Requests    Conflicts     Releases
------------------------ ------------ ------------ ------------
dc_awr_control                   4            0            0
dc_global_oids                   6            0            6
dc_histogram_defs            1,476            0        1,493
dc_object_ids                   72            0           73
dc_objects                     164            0          173
dc_profiles                      1            0            1
dc_segments                    149            7          141
dc_sequences                    94            5            0
outstanding_alerts              72           21            3
                  -------------------------------------------------------
```

```
Library Cache Activity  DB/Inst: SSD/ssd1  Snaps: 29-30
-> "Pct Misses"  should be very low

                     Get     Pct            Pin    Pct              Invali-
Namespace       Requests    Miss       Requests   Miss    Reloads    dations
--------------- --------- ------- ------------- ------ ---------- --------
BODY                  13    84.6            23   60.9          2        0
CLUSTER               24     8.3            39    5.1          0        0
INDEX                 23    95.7            27   81.5          0        0
JAVA DATA              1     0.0             0                 0        0
SQL AREA           3,297    10.3        11,849    5.1        119        0
TABLE/PROCEDURE      829    29.4         2,438   33.4        168        0
TRIGGER                1   100.0             2   50.0          0        0
                  -------------------------------------------------------
```

```
Library Cache Activity (RAC)  DB/Inst: SSD/ssd1  Snaps: 29-30

                 GES Lock      GES Pin     GES Pin   GES Inval GES Invali-
Namespace        Requests     Requests    Releases    Requests    dations
--------------- ------------ ------------ ------------ ----------- -----------
CLUSTER               39            2            2            2           0
INDEX                 27           22           22           22           0
TABLE/PROCEDURE    1,172          217          218           84           0
                  -------------------------------------------------------
```

```
SGA Memory Summary  DB/Inst: SSD/ssd1  Snap: 30

SGA regions                      Size in Bytes
------------------------------   ----------------
Database Buffers                   121,634,816
Fixed Size                             778,692
Redo Buffers                           524,288
Variable Size                      141,303,356
```

```
SGA breakdown difference  DB/Inst: SSD/ssd1  Snaps: 29-30

Pool    Name                        Begin value       End value     % Diff
------  --------------------------  ----------------  ----------------  -------
java    free memory                    2,808,320         2,808,320     0.00
java    joxlod exec hp                 5,346,432         5,346,432     0.00
java    joxs heap                        233,856           233,856     0.00
large   PX msg pool                      902,160           902,160     0.00
large   free memory                    3,292,144         3,292,144     0.00
shared  ASH buffers                    4,194,304         4,194,304     0.00
shared  FileOpenBlock                  3,978,620         3,978,620     0.00
shared  KGLS heap                      1,121,276         1,084,140    -3.31
shared  KQR L SO                          59,396            59,396     0.00
shared  KQR M PO                         966,152           957,392    -0.91
shared  KQR M SO                          59,908            59,908     0.00
shared  KQR S PO                         145,992           145,992     0.00
shared  KQR S SO                           7,168             7,168     0.00
shared  PL/SQL DIANA                     526,560           526,792     0.04
shared  PL/SQL MPCODE                    430,608           433,564     0.69
shared  PLS non-lib hp                    10,920            10,920     0.00
shared  PX subheap                       100,796           100,796     0.00
shared  event statistics per sess     25,092,340        25,092,340     0.00
shared  fixed allocation callback            416               416     0.00
shared  free memory                    3,265,908         3,349,172     2.55
shared  ges big msg buffers            3,979,396         3,979,396     0.00
shared  ges enqueues                   6,778,000         6,778,000     0.00
shared  ges reserved msg buffers       3,979,396         3,979,396     0.00
```

```
shared ges resources            3,794,384      3,794,384      0.00
shared joxlod exec hp             343,912        343,912      0.00
shared joxlod pcod hp              58,612         61,932      5.66
shared joxs heap                    4,220          4,220      0.00
shared library cache            9,528,188      9,505,184     -0.24
shared miscellaneous           50,199,332     50,220,004      0.04
shared object queue h               4,224          4,224      0.00
shared parameters                   1,044          1,044      0.00
shared partitioning d              84,372         83,452     -1.09
shared repository                  10,696         11,976     11.97
shared sessions                 5,069,744      5,069,744      0.00
shared sql area                 2,026,048      1,984,184     -2.07
shared table definiti                 696            696      0.00
shared trigger defini                 200            200      0.00
shared trigger inform               1,988          1,948     -2.01
shared type object de               4,304          4,304      0.00
       buffer_cache           121,634,816    121,634,816      0.00
       fixed_sga                 778,692        778,692      0.00
       log_buffer                524,288        524,288      0.00
          -------------------------------------------------------------
```

Resource Limit Stats DB/Inst: SSD/ssd1 Snap: 30

                    No data exists for this section of the report.
          ----

init.ora Parameters DB/Inst: SSD/ssd1 Snaps: 29-30

                                                         End value
Parameter Name   Begin value   (if different)
-------------------------- ------------------------   --------------
__db_cache_size   121634816
__java_pool_size   8388608
__large_pool_size   4194304
__shared_pool_size   125829120
background_dump_dest   /home/oracle/app/oracle/admin/ssd
cluster_database   TRUE
cluster_database_instances 2
compatible   10.1.0.2.0
control_files   /oracle2/oradata/ssd/control01.ct
core_dump_dest   /home/oracle/app/oracle/admin/ssd
db_block_size   8192
db_domain
db_file_multiblock_read_count 16
db_name   ssd
dispatchers   (PROTOCOL=TCP) (SERVICE=ssdXDB)
instance_number   1
job_queue_processes   10
open_cursors   300
pga_aggregate_target   356515840
processes   1000
remote_listener   LISTENERS_SSD
remote_login_passwordfile   EXCLUSIVE
sga_max_size   264241152
sga_target   264241152
spfile   /oracle2/oradata/ssd/spfilessd.or
thread   1
undo_management   AUTO
undo_tablespace   UNDOTBS1
user_dump_dest   /home/oracle/app/oracle/admin/ssd

Global Enqueue Statistics DB/Inst: SSD/ssd1 Snaps: 29-30

Statistic   Total   per Second   per Trans
---------------------------------- ------ ----------- -----------
acks for commit broadcast(actual)   0   0.0   0.0
acks for commit broadcast(logical   0   0.0   0.0
broadcast msgs on commit(actual)   0   0.0   0.0
broadcast msgs on commit(logical)   0   0.0   0.0
broadcast msgs on commit(wasted)   0   0.0   0.0
dynamically allocated gcs resourc   0   0.0   0.0
dynamically allocated gcs shadows   0   0.0   0.0
false posts waiting for scn acks   0   0.0   0.0
flow control messages received   0   0.0   0.0
flow control messages sent   0   0.0   0.0
gcs assume cvt   0   0.0   0.0
gcs assume no cvt   77   0.0   3.7
gcs ast xid   0   0.0   0.0
gcs blocked converts   197   0.1   9.4
gcs blocked cr converts   127   0.0   6.0
gcs compatible basts   0   0.0   0.0
gcs compatible cr basts (global)   0   0.0   0.0
gcs compatible cr basts (local)   9   0.0   0.4
```

**Example AWRRPT Report for 250 Megabyte SGA**          **195**
```

```
gcs cr basts to PIs                        0        0.0        0.0
gcs cr serve without current lock          0        0.0        0.0
gcs dbwr flush pi msgs                     51        0.0        2.4
gcs dbwr write request msgs                18        0.0        0.9
gcs error msgs                             0        0.0        0.0
gcs forward cr to pinged instance          0        0.0        0.0
gcs immediate (compatible) conver          2        0.0        0.1
gcs immediate (null) converts              9        0.0        0.4
gcs immediate cr (compatible) con          4        0.0        0.2
gcs immediate cr (null) converts           0        0.0        0.0
gcs indirect ast                          38        0.0        1.8
gcs lms flush pi msgs                      0        0.0        0.0
gcs lms write request msgs                31        0.0        1.5
gcs msgs process time(ms)                 30        0.0        1.4
gcs msgs received                        694        0.2       33.0
gcs out-of-order msgs                      0        0.0        0.0
gcs pings refused                          0        0.0        0.0
gcs queued converts                        0        0.0        0.0
gcs recovery claim msgs                    0        0.0        0.0
gcs refuse xid                             0        0.0        0.0
gcs regular cr                             0        0.0        0.0
gcs retry convert request                  0        0.0        0.0
gcs side channel msgs actual              31        0.0        1.5
gcs side channel msgs logical            313        0.1       14.9
gcs undo cr                                0        0.0        0.0
gcs write notification msgs                8        0.0        0.4
gcs writes refused                         1        0.0        0.0
ges msgs process time(ms)                 53        0.0        2.5
ges msgs received                      7,542        2.1      359.1
global posts dropped                       0        0.0        0.0
global posts queue time                    0        0.0        0.0
global posts queued                        0        0.0        0.0
global posts requested                     0        0.0        0.0
global posts sent                          0        0.0        0.0
implicit batch messages received          44        0.0        2.1
implicit batch messages sent              57        0.0        2.7
lmd msg send time(ms)                      0        0.0        0.0
lms(s) msg send time(ms)                   0        0.0        0.0
messages flow controlled                 655        0.2       31.2
messages queue sent actual             5,445        1.5      259.3
messages queue sent logical            5,537        1.5      263.7
messages received actual               7,121        2.0      339.1
```

Global Enqueue Statistics DB/Inst: SSD/ssd1 Snaps: 29-30

Statistic	Total	per Second	per Trans
messages received logical	8,236	2.3	392.2
messages sent directly	1,831	0.5	87.2
messages sent indirectly	2,037	0.6	97.0
messages sent not implicit batche	5,388	1.5	256.6
messages sent pbatched	6,165	1.7	293.6
msgs causing lmd to send msgs	4,358	1.2	207.5
msgs causing lms(s) to send msgs	84	0.0	4.0
msgs received queue time (ms)	46	0.0	2.2
msgs received queued	8,237	2.3	392.2
msgs sent queue time (ms)	60	0.0	2.9
msgs sent queue time on ksxp (ms)	1,299	0.4	61.9
msgs sent queued	5,528	1.5	263.2
msgs sent queued on ksxp	7,287	2.0	347.0
process batch messages received	2,140	0.6	101.9
process batch messages sent	4,626	1.3	220.3

Global CR Served Stats DB/Inst: SSD/ssd1 Snaps: 29-30

Statistic	Total
CR Block Requests	116
CURRENT Block Requests	27
Data Block Requests	116
Undo Block Requests	0
TX Block Requests	27
Current Results	143
Private results	0
Zero Results	0
Disk Read Results	0
Fail Results	0
Fairness Down Converts	19
Fairness Clears	0
Free GC Elements	0
Flushes	0
Flushes Queued	0
Flush Queue Full	0

```
Flush Max Time (us)                      0
Light Works                              0
Errors                                   0
      ------------------------------------------------------------

Global CURRENT Served Stats  DB/Inst: SSD/ssd1  Snaps: 29-30
-> Pins    = CURRENT Block Pin Operations
-> Flushes = Redo Flush before CURRENT Block Served Operations
-> Writes  = CURRENT Block Fusion Write Operations

Statistic         Total   % <1ms  % <10ms % <100ms   % <1s   % <10s
----------  ------------- -------- -------- -------- -------- --------
Pins                169   100.00     0.00     0.00     0.00     0.00
Flushes               0     0.00     0.00     0.00     0.00     0.00
Writes               55    94.55     5.45     0.00     0.00     0.00
      ------------------------------------------------------------

Global Cache Transfer Stats  DB/Inst: SSD/ssd1  Snaps: 29-30

              No data exists for this section of the report.
      ------------------------------------------------------------

End of Report
```

About Mike Ault

Mike Ault is one of the leading names in Oracle technology. The author of more than 20 Oracle books and hundreds of articles in national publications, Mike Ault has five Oracle Masters Certificates and was the first popular Oracle author with his landmark book Oracle7 Administration and Management. Mike also wrote several of the Exam Cram books, and enjoys a reputation as a leading author and Oracle consultant.

Mike started working with computers in 1979 right out of a stint in the Nuclear Navy. He began working with Oracle in 1990 and has since become a World Renowned Oracle expert. Mike is currently a Senior Technical Management Consultant and has two wonderful daughters. Mike is kept out of trouble by his wife of 29 years, Susan.

About Don Burleson

Don Burleson is one of the world's top Oracle Database experts with more than 20 years of full-time DBA experience. He specializes in creating database architectures for very large online databases and he has worked with some of the world's most powerful and complex systems.

A former Adjunct Professor, Don Burleson has written 32 books, published more than 100 articles in National Magazines, and serves as Editor-in-Chief of Oracle Internals and Senior Consulting Editor for DBAZine and Series Editor for Rampant TechPress. Don is a popular lecturer and teacher and is a frequent speaker at OracleWorld and other international database conferences.

As a leading corporate database consultant, Don has worked with numerous Fortune 500 corporations creating robust database architectures for mission-critical systems. Don is also a noted expert on eCommerce systems, and has been instrumental in the development of numerous Web-based systems that support thousands of concurrent users.

In addition to his services as a consultant, Don also is active in charitable programs to aid visually impaired individuals. Don pioneered a technique for delivering tiny pigmy horses as guide animals for the blind and manages a non-profit corporation called the Guide Horse Foundation dedicated to providing Guide horses to blind people free-of-charge. The Web Site for The Guide Horse Foundation is www.guidehorse.org.

About Mike Reed

When he first started drawing, Mike Reed drew just to amuse himself. It wasn't long, though, before he knew he wanted to be an artist. Today he does illustrations for children's books, magazines, catalogs, and ads.

He also teaches illustration at the College of Visual Art in St. Paul, Minnesota. Mike Reed says, "Making pictures is like acting — you can paint yourself into the action." He often paints on the computer, but he also draws in pen and ink and paints in acrylics. He feels that learning to draw well is the key to being a successful artist.

Mike is regarded as one of the nation's premier illustrators and is the creator of the popular "Flame Warriors" illustrations at www.flamewarriors.com, a website devoted to Internet insults. "To enter his Flame Warriors site is sort of like entering a hellish Sesame Street populated by Oscar the Grouch and 83 of his relatives." – Los Angeles Times. (http://redwing.hutman.net/%7Emreed/warriorshtm/lat.htm)

Mike Reed has always enjoyed reading. As a young child, he liked the Dr. Seuss books. Later, he started reading biographies and war stories. One reason why he feels lucky to be an illustrator is because he can listen to books on tape while he works. Mike is available to provide custom illustrations for all manner of publications at reasonable prices. Mike can be reached at www.mikereedillustration.com.